PERSPECTIVES ON PENTECOSTALISM:
Case Studies from the Caribbean and Latin America

Stephen D. Glazier

LIBRARY
McCORMICK THEOLOGICAL SEMINARY
1100 EAST 55th STREET
CHICAGO, ILLINOIS 6061℠

University Press of America™

Copyright © 1980 by

University Press of America, Inc.

4710 Auth Place, S.E., Washington, D.C. 20023

All rights reserved
Printed in the United States of America
ISBN: 0-8191-1071-X (Case)
0-8191-1072-8 (Perfect)

BR
1644.5
.C37
P47

Library of Congress Catalog Card Number: 80-7815

ACKNOWLEDGMENTS

This volume could not exist without help and encouragement from many scholars. In addition to my contributors, I wish to thank Angelina Pollak-Eltz, Felicitas D. Goodman, Donald E. Curry and Leslie G. Desmangles for their comments and suggestions.

My wife, Rosemary C. Glazier, assisted me in a variety of editorial tasks including subject and name indices. Janet Carson typed a good part of the final manuscript.

CONTENTS

PREFACE   vii

PART 1.   INTRODUCTION

    The Paradoxical Growth of Pentecostalism, by Luise Margolies   1

PART 2.   THE CARIBBEAN

    Pentecostalism in Haiti: Healing and Hierarchy, by Frederick J. Conway   7

    Modernization and the Pentecostal Movement in Jamaica, by William Wedenoja   27

    Pentecostalism in Puerto Rican Society, by Anthony L. LaRuffa   49

    Pentecostal Exorcism and Modernization in Trinidad, West Indies, by Stephen D. Glazier   67

PART 3.   LATIN AMERICA

    Pentecostalism and Development: the Colombian Case, by Cornelia Butler Flora.   81

    The Power of Pentecostalism in a Belizean Village, by Donna Birdwell-Pheasant   95

    Pentecostalism: A Revolutionary or Conservative Movement, by Judith Chambliss Hoffnagel   111

    Capitalism and Religion at the Periphery: Pentecostalism and Umbanda in Brazil, by Gary Nigel Howe   125

    Catholic Pentecostalism: A New Word in a New World, by Thomas J. Chordas   143

PART 4. CONCLUSIONS

    Pentecostalism: Christianity and
    Reputation, by Frank E. Manning   177

CONTRIBUTORS   189

INDEX OF NAMES   191

INDEX OF SUBJECTS   195

PREFACE

These eleven papers, seven of which were prepared originally for the 1977 annual meeting of the American Anthropological Association, focus on the growth of Pentecostalism in the Caribbean and Latin America. Cases from Puerto Rico, Trinidad, Haiti, Jamaica, Colombia, Belize and Brazil are included herein.

Each contributor seems to advocate a different avenue of investigation for this phenomena and the issues raised in this volume are far from resolved. Whether Pentecostalism is to be understood in terms of imperialism, dependency patterns, or as Professor Wedenoja has postulated, a widespread cultural and religious "syncretism," the complexities are enormous.

Pentecostalism is a loosely structured phenomena and if (as it is sometimes tempting to suggest) there are as many "Pentecostalisms" as there are Pentecostal congregations, diversity within this volume is not surprising. My own feeling, not readily discernable from my essay, is that Pentecostalism and its growth cannot be explained solely in terms of imperialism because it is often difficult to determine where imperialist forces lie; that is, it is hard to say exactly who is influencing and/or exploiting whom? If Pentecostalism is modifying indigenous beliefs and practices so too are these beliefs influencing Pentecostalism. A one-sided transactional analysis is necessarily incomplete and it appears to make little difference how unequal the relationships being studied or where major forces of production within a society are located.

Contributors have, for the most part, chosen to underplay "exotic" aspects of the faith and emphasized its influence on everyday economic, social and political affairs. Their concern with the quotidian is a fruitful one, and as these papers demonstrate, may add significantly to our understanding of the rise of Pentecostalism in the Caribbean and other parts of South America.

-- Stephen D. Glazier
Storrs, Connecticut
January 28, 1980

THE PARADOXICAL GROWTH OF PENTECOSTALISM

Luise Margolies
Instituto Venezolano de Investigaciones
Cientificas

Despite the different approaches to the subject of Pentecostalism and modernization, the papers presented in this symposium amply demonstrate that single-factor explanations for the recent and rapid growth of the Pentecostal movement are insufficient. The papers barely touch on the ecstatic experience inherent in being "born again" and de-emphasize the organizational aspects of the movement, yet all discuss the particular socio-cultural conditions which have favored its development—often to the detriment of orthodox religious activities. Whether one has recourse to the rubric of modernization or deals more specifically with industrialization, urbanization, proletarianization or capitalist development, it is obvious that the seemingly random emergence of Pentecostalism is irrefutably correlated with massive social changes occurring in today's developing countries. Setting the course of the movement in the context of historical circumstances, nation by nation—as these papers have done—is an important step in eliminating rigid cause-and-effect relationships.

Implicit in each of the papers is the close association between modernization and the transition from agrarian to urban society. Undoubtedly rural-urban migration, intra-regional migration, and out-migration have all contributed to the ease with which the Pentecostal movement has spread. Hoffnagel states this most explicitly for Brazil by noting that "the phenomenal growth of Pentecostalism has taken place during a period marked by an increased pace of industrialization, a rationalization of export agriculture and a demographic shift from rural to urban areas." Migrants are seen to have been especially likely candidates for Pentecostal churches in Colombia (Flora), Brazil (Howe), and Haiti (Conway), while in Jamaica, return migrants were often instrumental in organizing Pentecostal groups (Wedenoja). Why do migrants make good potential converts? Without necessarily resorting to such polemical consequences of change as "dislocation" (Flora), "marginality" or "alienation" (Birdwell), these persons by the very act of migrating, are proponents for change. In the specific case histories presented here, the Pentecostal Church has been seen as a logical substitute for the extended family ties temporarily or perhaps permanently severed by migration. Furthermore, behavioral patterns in the new Church are based on the same norms of reciprocity and mutual aid inherent in relations among kin and fictive kin. The replication of one's social network in the religious sphere through the joining of a surrogate family is considerably facilitated, given the scarcity of formal organizations and other institutional supports. According to Howe, Pentecostalism flourishes where "traditional supports have been eroded without provision of either sufficient resources for individuals to cope independently with life crises or formal institutional supports for individuals in the form of social welfare agencies." Of course, migration alone is not responsible for bridging new avenues of social articulation. Natural disasters and other unforseen events can also have the same result. Birdwell, for example, documents the early growth of the Seventh Day Adventists in the wake of severe population losses. Country by country, then, Pentecostalism has been shown to be not simply some aberrant activity, practiced fanatically or even surreptitiously, but a momentous movement whose implications for national development are first being explored.

Perhaps because the emphasis in these papers is on the movement per se as an index of change, the role of faith healing in individual commitment to the Church is summarily treated. Both Conway and Glazier demonstrate in their analyses of single congregations that faith healing constitutes the essential element of the Pentecostal sermon. Much as the saints are invoked in the Catholic Church upon consultation with orthodox medical practioners, conversion to Pentecostalism serves as a backup mechanism in the face of traditional therapeutic failures. Does faith healing represent a syncretic variant of older curing practices, "an innovation within the traditional system" as Conway notes, or does Pentecostal exorcism actually foster more "rational" approaches to dealing with the supernatural, as Glazier claims? Certainly this question cannot be answered without examining why persons convert. If they are simply looking for the most effective way of weathering a personal illness, then faith healing would seem to be the crux of Pentecostal rituals. But once they become committed converts, regardless of the initial reason for recruitment, then faith healing must be placed in the context of a compelling doctrine which promises to transcend other ideologies in reshaping one's personal values. Only then can we begin to understand the phenomenal appeal that Pentecostalism has experienced in recent years. As Pollak-Eltz has demonstrated in her ongoing study of Venezuelan Pentecostalism, the movement encompasses numerous splinter groups which differ substantially in what they provide for their clients (1976). Unless we sort out these diversities, it is futile to attempt to explain the extraordinary success of the movement.

    Paradoxically, on the individual level, Pentecostalism seems to offer a pragmatic variation of customary healing practices, while on the organizational level, Pentecostalism has been seen as a movement for radical change. All of the papers have grappled with this paradox and exemplify the lack of consensus on this pivotal point. At one extreme, Pentecostalism is considered a spontaneous revolutionary movement whose impressive growth is inextricably linked to the rupture of anachronistic social forms and the consequent socioeconomic modernization of the last few decades. This position is best represented by Wedenoja who sees Pentecostal affiliation as "a symbolic expression of one's acceptance of and commitment to a new society," as well as the foundation for "a unified national culture based on a developing middle class and embodying a uniform set of values for all." At the other end of the spectrum, Hoffnagel treats Pentecostalism as a decidedly conservative phenomenon, tending to strengthen rather than weaken traditional forms of social organization." Although the movement has grown by erratic leaps which parallel the quickened pace of industrialization, Hoffnagel demonstrates that the congregation acts as a type of corporate community which replicates the paternalistic social hierarchy of the old plantation system. The other papers take a more cautious stance in which syncretic change must be balanced against the movement's potential for genuine institutional innovations. Thus, Birdwell and Flora believe that the movement's potential for social change has yet to be fulfilled. Conway notes that the administrative organization of the Pentecostal churches represents a considerable break from the past despite the parallels between Vodoun and faith healing, while Glazier feels that healing sessions, precisely because of the total religious context, provide new alternatives in the process of modernization.

As Gerlach has noted, most studies of religious movements stress equilibrium, while few consider deviations from the norm as indicators of radical or even revolutionary change (1974: 698-699). Certainly, Pentecostalism has something for a variety of potential disciples and crosses religious, class, and generational barriers. But at the same time, by demanding adherence to the strict principles that affect personal behavior, the movement constitutes a fundamental departure from traditional values. This symposium is a refreshing step in less travelled directions precisely because it rejects the equilibrium model. By no means have the authors concurred on the role of Pentecostalism in the modernization process, yet all have recognized that it must be set squarely in the context of broader socio-cultural phenomena in order to study its exaggerated growth.

REFERENCES CITED

Gerlach, Luther P.
   1974   Pentecostalism: Revolution or Counter-Revolution: In Religious Movements in Contemporary America. Zaretsky, Irving and Mark Leone, eds. Princeton: Princeton University Press. Pp. 669-699.

Pollak-Eltz, Angelina
   1976   El pentecostalismo catolico en Venezuela. Caracas: Sic 384:172-177.

PENTECOSTALISM IN HAITI: HEALING AND HIERARCHY

Frederick J. Conway

American University

Introduction

Haiti, the oldest and most populated nation in the Caribbean, has had a singular social history. In the eighteenth century, it became France's most profitable colony--a profit based on one of the most brutal slave systems in the Americas. What makes Haiti unique is that its Revolution was the only massively successful slave rebellion in the New World. Haiti became the second American republic in 1804. The plantation system had been largely destroyed and most of the former slaves settled in the interior areas of the country to become what Mintz (1966: xxii) called a "reconstituted yeomanry." Haiti was diplomatically isolated by the European powers and the United States, who feared that their own slaves would be inspired by the Haitian victory. During this period of isolation, the Haitian yeomanry developed its own national culture, with distinctive patterns of agriculture, family structure and religion. The diplomatic isolation ended in the second half of the nineteenth century, which introduced a period of political and economic interference, culminating in the invasion of Haiti by United Stated marines in 1915. The United States maintained direct political control over Haiti until 1934 and direct financial control until 1946.

Thus Haiti has experienced an unusual degree of isolation as well as interference by foreign powers. This combination of isolation and subjugation has been an important factor in the formation of many aspects of Haitian culture, which must be taken into account in the discussion of Pentecostalism in Haiti. The analysis which follows is concerned with both the "internal" and "external" aspects of Haitian Pentecostalism. The "internal" aspect of Pentecostalism in Haiti includes its curative function and its fit with the traditional religious system; the "external" aspect is the organizational links with the outside world and the ideology in which these links are made. In brief: healing and hierarchy.[1]

The Haitian Religious Context

Pentecostalism in Haiti can only be understood in the context of Vodoun, Catholicism and the various Protestant denominations there. The traditional religion of Haiti is a complex of Vodoun and Catholicism. Vodoun involves the worship of spirits called loua or (Fr. mystères).[2] These spirits are inherited by families; the inheritance is bilateral and individuals speak of their "mother's loua" and "father's loua." The numerous loua are believed to protect the family against misfortune, but they may also punish a family which displeases them. The relationship between a family and its loua is renewed in periodic rituals in which the spirits are "fed" with prescribed foods and drink, as well as with dance and song. During these and other Vodoun rituals, Haitians may enter trance states and become possessed by the loua. In such a state the trance subject takes on the "personality" of a loua, acting as if he or she were the spirit.

The loua are manifested principally through the bodies of humans rather then through natural processes outside of humans (Murray 1977: 512 ff). As we have seen, loua are believed to incarnate themselves in the bodies of humans, temporarily displacing the human individual's personality and taking complete control of his or her body. The loua also make themselves known in dreams. When they are angry, the loua are believed to express their displeasure most frequently by making a family member ill. In Vodounist belief, the loua have some limited influence over natural processes outside of the human body; but only rarely are they invoked as explanations for climatic or agricultural events. In addition to the loua, Vodounists also believe in a number of fearsome supernatural beings (for example, captured souls, purchased sprites, vampire-like humans). Like the loua, these beings are manifested primarily in their effects on the human body. They are feared mostly for the illnesses they are believed to cause.

When Vodounists become ill, they often consult a specialist (the male houngan or female manbo), who divines the cause of the illness. Illnesses are categorized as (1) natural (or more literally, "God-sent"); as (2) caused by angry loua or ancestral ghosts; or as (3) caused by malevolent agents, usually human, who manipulate supernatural powers. If the illness is determined to be "supernatural" rather than "God-sent," the Vodoun specialist will mediate with the displeased family loua or ancestral ghost seen to be responsible, or will counterattack the malevolent agent. Initiation into a Vodoun cult group is a further means of treatment. All of these services must be paid for, and can become very expensive.

The Vodoun specialist claims only to be able to treat illnesses which are "supernatural." Against the majority of illnesses, those "sent by God," the specialist is admittedly powerless. The power of the loua and of the Vodoun specialists, then, is limited. This very limitation, however, is one of the strengths of the traditional religion in its functioning as a system of health practice. The belief system provides a variety of alternative etiologies and therapies, and it allows for a degree of experimentation in the treatment of illness. The houngan and manbo cannot cure every illness, but their successes and failures can be accounted for. If the Vodoun specialist fails in his or her treatment, alternative treatments can be pursued without violating the logic of the Vodoun belief system.

In addition to a recognition of the limitations of the loua and the Vodoun specialists there is a degree of ambivalence towards them for many

Haitians. The specialist has powers with which to cure and relieve other misfortunes. But these same powers can also be used for malevolent purposes. Furthermore, it is commonly believed that a number of specialists are charlatans who dupe their clients. The loua, too, are the objects of ambivalent attitudes. While the loua generally protect their human "children," they are also the cause of misfortune. If in some ways the relationship between families and their inherited loua are contractual, it is not a contract that is freely entered by the human partners. And in any case, the degree of protection that the loua can provide is limited, as we have seen. The loua have not protected most Haitians from poverty, illiteracy or the risk of debilitating disease.

The loua and other supernatural beings in the Vodoun belief system are placed within a Catholic cosmology which makes them subordinate to God, (Fr.) Bon-Dieu. For those who "serve the loua," Vodoun is not separate from Catholicism. When asked to identify their religion, Vodounists respond that they are Catholic. The use of the word "Vodoun" to describe a discrete religious system would make little sense to a rural Haitian. The Vodounist is less troubled by doctrinal contradictions between Vodoun and Catholicism than the orthodox Catholic might be. In part this is due to a lack of familiarity with orthodox Catholic doctrine and in part to the fact that possibly conflicting elements in the traditional religion are experienced in separate contexts. The loua are categorized as a type of angel or saint who exercise some independence from Bon-Dieu, but are ultimately subject to him.

Historically, the administration of the worship of Bon-Dieu has been controlled by foreign clergy, whose interests coincided with those of the Haitian upper class. As an institution, the Catholic Church is still perceived as foreign, often as specifically French. The attitude of the Catholic hierarchy towards Vodounist belief and practice has ranged from indifference and tolerance to extreme hostility. The Catholic clergy have conducted a number of anti-Vodoun campaigns, most notably in the 1940's. The very existence of Catholicism in Haiti as a foreign institution and an elite form of worship tended to brand the indigenous Vodoun as inferior. The Catholic clergy allied themselves with the Haitian elite, who wished to be associated with French "civilization" and to be disassociated from African "barbarism," represented by Vodoun. The practice of Vodoun has been associated with the non-elite classes in Haiti, especially with the large rural population. Catholicism tends to reaffirm Haiti's position in the world of nations and the yeomanry's position within Haiti's highly stratified social system. And yet, this denigration of Vodoun can only be said to be partial, because Vodounists themselves only partially accept it. Within the framework of the traditional religion it is possible to "reject the loua" and become a "pure Catholic" (Fr. catholique franc). For most Vodounists, however, Catholic and Vodounist elements are too thoroughly integrated with each other to be meaningfully separated. Thus only a few Vodounists have become "pure Catholics."

For the Vodounist, the Catholic Church represents the "external" aspect of the traditional religion. The Catholic Church has been an important link to both the Haitian state (providing identification papers and administering marriage) and to the outside world. The institutional links are reflected on the ideological level as well. In contrast to the all-powerful Bon-Dieu, who is recognized and worshipped on an international scale, the loua are limited in power and confined in their influence to the Haitian scene. The relationship of Vodoun to Catholicism is both a product of and a metaphor for the place of the Vodounist within Haiti and the larger world.

Like Catholicism in Haiti, Protestantism is perceived as international in scope. Protestantism is seen primarily as North American, and, in fact, it is largely the enterprise of mission organizations from the United States. There has been a limited Protestant presence in Haiti since the early nineteenth century. In the aftermath of the United States occupation of Haiti, this presence has grown to the point where Protestants may number as much as 15% of the population.[3] A fairly wide spectrum of Protestant denominations is active in Haiti. They range from the Methodists and Episcopalians to a large number of Baptist organizations to a variety of Pentecostal groups.

The belief system of Haitian Pentecostalism excludes both Catholicism and Vodoun. With its militant ideology of conversion, Protestantism involves a rejection of reliance on the loua and the Vodoun specialist, replacing them with an exclusive faith in the power of Bon-Dieu. Protestants summon images of confrontation and power when referring to Vodoun and Catholicism. Military imagery is common, and a number of Pentecostal congregations call themselves "The Army," envisioning themselves as joined by platoons of angels in their combat against the loua and the houngan. The most frequently told stories about conversion to Protestantism involve a struggle between a Protestant leader and a Vodoun specialist, the one using Bon-Dieu, the other using the loua, to effect a cure or resolve some other problem.

Protestant converts continue to accept possession by loua as a fact of everyday life. They even continue to believe that the loua can cure illnesses and bring good fortune, at least in the short run. But the loua themselves are reinterpreted as evil spirits, devils who are the followers of Satan. The sharp distinction that Vodounists make between family loua and evil spirits is eliminated. Protestants tend to use the term "evil spirits" (Fr. mauvais esprits) rather than "loua." For many converts this shift in terminology is not difficult because they have had bad experiences with the loua. These experiences usually stem from a failure or unwillingness to "feed" the loua or from a failure to be cured of an illness believed to be caused by a loua of by a human agent who might be stopped by a loua.

Haitian Protestants take a rhetorical stance of firm rejection of the loua. Yet their attitude towards the loua is ambiguous. Protestants maintain that the loua are "nothing" and that the Vodoun specialists are all charlatans, their work a mere sham. At the same time, Protestants tell stories in which the loua and the Vodoun specialists are their powerful adversaries. In fact, no one in Haitian communities proclaims more publicly the existence and power of the loua and of other Vodoun forces than do the Protestants. The traditional belief system and the anxieties it provokes are used by Protestants to reinforce fidelity within their own groups, since one who "falls" back to Vodoun after conversion to Protestantism may incur the deep wrath of the loua for having abandoned them in the first place.

Pentecostalism in Haiti is particularly interesting because, like Vodoun, it emphasizes trance behavior and spirit possession beliefs. The Pentecostals are characterized by what Haitians call (Fr.) manifestations, that is trance behavior and glossolalia. A central tenet of Pentecostalism is that this behavior is a manifestation of the Holy Spirit. In addition to their belief in possession by the Holy Spirit, Pentecostals are distinguished from other Protestants by their use of drums, hand-clapping and dance. Pentecostals see these activities as making services "hot," providing an atmosphere conducive to the descent of the Holy Spirit. Non-Pentecostal Protestants tend to condemn these practices, as well as belief in possession by the Holy Spirit.

We have seen that Haitians are familiar with trance behavior and spirit possession beliefs. The manifestations seen in the Pentecostal churches are not wholly alien to Haitians. They are variations on a tried theme rather than startling innovations. The manifestations are seen as both similar to possession by the loua and in competition with it. The most important difference is the Pentecostal claim that the behavior is caused by the Holy Spirit. The trance performances of Pentecostals

are not particularly impressive in comparison with
those of Vodounists. This has led some Vodounists
to scoff that the Pentecostals are possessed by
nothing more than minor loua or that they are in-
dulging in histrionics. Pentecostals, too, believe
that glossolalia can be caused by loua who attempt
to disrupt the life of a congregation by imitating
the Holy Spirit. Trance behavior clearly distinguishes Pentecostals from other Protestants and is
the principal criterion by which Haitians categor-
ize Protestants. However, Pentecostal trance behavior cannot stand alone as the central attraction for prospective converts. Rather, the manifestations are a sign of spiritual power whose
efficacy lies elsewhere--in the healing functions
of the Pentecostal congregation.

Pentecostal Healing

"Divine healing" (Fr. guérison divine) was a
primary activity of all of the Pentecostal congregations which were observed during fifteen months
of fieldwork in Haiti. Pentecostalism offers
treatment for illness in three forms: prayer,
laying on of hands, and conversion itself. More
than three fourths of the Pentecostals interviewed reported that they had converted on the occasion of an illness, either their own or that of
a parent or child. Many converted only after one
or more expensive but unsuccessful trips to the
Vodoun specialist. For many, conversion to Pentecostalism represented a last resort after their
supernatural and financial resources were ex-
hausted.

The Haitian Creole verb "to convert" (konvéti)
does not carry the same meaning as in English. It
can mean to change religious affiliation or belief;
but it may also mean simply to have a religious
group pray over one, with the implication that one
will join the group. Konvéti does not necessarily
imply conviction of the truth of a religious doctrine. One informant was unconscious when she was
"converted" in this way. Others may be unwilling
to be "converted," but are unable to defend them-

selves. For conversion to be an effective means of "divine healing," however, it must involve a new relationship of the convert to Bon-Dieu, mediated through the spiritual power of the Pentecostal congregation. The convert must devote him- or herself to the congregation, giving up services for the family loua and visits to the Vodoun specialist. The convert must also give up extra-legal marital unions, drinking, smoking and gambling.

Conversion is not the only point at which Pentecostalism become involved with health practice. If it were, converts might return to Vodoun practice as soon as the immediate health crisis which generated the conversion passed. (Some indeed do just that.) Prayer for the cure of illness is a part of every service. It is customary at the end of prayer services for those who are ill to be prayed over by the pastor or by a person in the congregation believed to have the gift of healing. Such prayer is considered to be not only curative but prophylactic as well. Indeed, most Pentecostal ritual activity is designed to give its adherents continuous protection against their enemies, human and spiritual. Pentecostals also visit fellow congregants in their homes when they are sick in order to pray over them. Unlike the health services of the Vodoun specialist, these services are offered free of charge. The congregant is asked to make a small weekly contribution to the church organization, but no one is asked to pay for specific services rendered.

While other Protestant groups also pray for the sick and attract converts who seek relief from illness, they usually do not place the same emphasis on healing as the Pentecostals. Since there is usually more than one type of Protestant group in any given locale, differences in style and emphasis are crucial in the competition to attract converts. The Pentecostals make their claim of having the power to heal as a part of their claim to have received the "gifts of the Holy Spirit." "Divine healing" is only one of these gifts. The most distinctive of them, of course, is "speaking in tongues," Glossolalia in a **Pentecostal** congregant is a sign that the group as a whole has been blessed with the gifts of the Holy Spirit, one of which is the gift of healing. When Pentecostals describe their conversion, they usually speak of the greater power (Fr. force or puissance) of the Pentecostals in comparison with other Protestants and especially with Vodoun. Pentecostals say that spiritual power can only be obtained from "evil spirits" or from God. Pentecostalism is attractive because it is perceived as bestowing greater power on the individual. Ideas of moral superiority are secondary in Pentecostals' discussions of their religion. In a sense, the moral disciplines of Pentecostalism are seen as instruments for obtaining force rather than as ends in themselves. However, it is the congregation, not merely certain individuals within it, which is "sanctified" with force. Even though the Holy Spirit only is "manifested" in certain individuals through glossolalia (about 10% of the congregations observed), Pentecostals believe that the blessing is shared by the entire congregation. The message is clear: the Holy Spirit can protect the individual, but only if he or she joins with other members of the group in prayer, song and fasting.

A physiological analysis of the effectiveness of Pentecostal healing rituals is outside of the scope of this study. However, Pentecostal converts often report that they have been "cured" (Fr. gueri) after their conversion. They are certainly encouraged to do so. Testifying to the intervention of Bon-Dieu in the fortunes of daily life are an important part of almost every Pentecostal religious service. Pentecostals strive to reinforce the belief of their fellow congregants in the healing power of God. Conversion or a healing service after conversion may only bring temporary relief from an illness. This is probably frequently the case when an individual converts during an episode of malaria, a widespread illness in Haiti. In part, relapses or subsequent illnesses may be denied by the Pentecostal; in part they can be rationalized as "tests" by God of the fidelity of the convert. Nevertheless, one of the greatest challenges to the Pentecostal ideology is what Gerlach and Hine (1968:34) call the "ideal-real" gap. The failure to be definitively cured may be accompanied by cognitive dissonance. Leon Festinger and his colleagues maintained that rationalization and denial cannot eliminate cognitive dissonance completely. "But there is a way in which the remaining dissonance can be reduced. If more and more people can be persuaded that the system of belief is correct, then clearly, after all, it must be correct" (Festinger et al. 1964: 24). The aggressive stance and active proselytizing of the Pentecostals may be seen as functioning in part to reduce the dissonance generated by the failure of illnesses and other misfortunes to disappear completely from their lives. Proselytizing is certainly essential to the recruitment of converts. But the images of power and confrontation used by Pentecostals in their preaching may be produced even more for those who are already converted than for prospective converts. These images are obviously an important factor in attracting converts. But they are generated and maintained by individuals who have already committed themselves to Pentecostalism, individuals who have inevitably suffered some disappointment in their new religion. It is the certitude of the Pentecostal ideology which is its greatest strength, as Gerlach and Hine (1968: 35) have noted. The sense of certitude exhibited by Pentecostals is supported by their trance behavior, as we have seen. The rhetorical stance and trance behavior of the Pentecostals may not have convinced all Haitians of the unassailable validity of Pentecostalism, but they have drawn a considerable number away from the traditional religious patterns.

If certitude is the strength of Haitian Pentecostalism in its functioning as a system of health practice, the contrast with Haitian Vodoun is striking. As we have seen, the strength of the Vodoun belief system is the limitation set on the power of the loua and the Vodoun specialist. Because of this limitation, as well as of the ambivalence felt toward the _loua_ and the Vodoun specialists, Vodoun admits of alternative systems of health practice and religious observance. The two belief systems, then, handle disappointments differently: Vodoun through flexibility and Pentecostalism through the claim of establishing a rigid and impermeable barrier between the congregant and the powers of Vodoun. It will be remembered that the traditional religion offers a mechanism for rejecting the _loua_ and healing illness through the acceptance of "pure" Catholicism. However, "pure" Catholicism has not been notably successful in comparison with Vodoun because the Catholic Church has not been able to communicate the sense that it can offer protection from angry _loua_ and other supernatural powers.

In addition to its healing rituals, supported by active proselytizing and by the demonstrations of spiritual power manifested in glossolalia, Pentecostalism differs from the traditional religion in providing an organizational base--an administrative hierarchy--which has the promise of providing converts with additional benefits. This organization structure is discussed in the next section.

Pentecostal Hierarchy

The administrative structure of many Pentecostal groups is a feature which is shared with other Protestant organizations. In Protestant mission churches, the administrative structure can be fairly elaborate, culminating in a foreign mission board, usually in the United States. One of the congregations studied in Haiti, the Bethesda Assembly, can serve as an example here. The Bethesda Assembly began as a small, local Pentecostal group principally involved in healing. Its founder, a man who had been converted in the capital and later returned to his village with his wife, became a healer of some local renown. Some year after establishing his group, the founder encountered an American missionary (through his Pentecostal contacts in the city) and persuaded him to build a church for the group. The cinderblock and corrugated iron Bethesda church is now the most imposing building in the rural village.

The Bethesda Assembly has been Successful in local eyes because it has managed to attract foreign interest. Having some connection with the hierarchy of the mission is believed to bring material benefits to the members of the congregation. This is certainly true. The Bethesda church maintains a school, provides inexpensive weddings and occasionally distributes gifts of food. However, there have been some disappointments. For example, one man agreed to become the deacon of the Bethesda Assembly, partly in hope of receiving some financial remuneration for his work. After a year in the office, and after having invested in a suit and a pair of shoes, he complained that he had received nothing. The expansion of the school did not create new jobs for local residents, as some had expected. Rather, teachers from outside the village who were known to the mission administration were brought in.

At a Sunday school session in another Pentecostal congregation in the same village one week, the congregation was memorizing a verse from the New Testament. The verse in question (Matthew 7:8) was "He who seeks shall find...." In French this verse reads, "Celui qui cherche trouvera...." Several members of the congregation, mixing French and Haitian Creole, repeated the verse as "Celui qui chef trouvera...," which can be translated as, "He who is the boss shall find...." This incident underlined a common perception about the administrartive hierarchy: that it helps those who have a place in it, but not those who have none.

This is certainly true for the pastors of Protestant congregations. Bible school has provided them with not only a Fundamentalist religious education, but also with the social skills which will enable them to make successful contacts with foreigners. English is the most important of these skills. The disappointed deacon of the Bethesda

Assembly said that if only he spoke English he could explain his situation to the American missionary who supervised the church, and everything would be arranged.

When the Bethesda Assembly became a mission church, its founder was superseded by a licensed pastor. This man was said to have been a good pastor because he had connections with many Americans and was able to obtain many gifts for the local congregation. However, he had his own personal aspirations, and used his connections to obtain a position in the United States. The current pastor, the fourth the Bethesda Assembly has had in a decade, is a young man who is still in Bible school. He succeeded his own brother, who was transferred to another community. The older brother used his position to obtain the Bethesda Assembly vacancy for the young student. The local founder of the Bethesda group objected to this nepotism and was driven from the church. Undaunted, he left with a small group of loyal followers, promising them that with the help of the Holy Spirit he would find them an even richer American than the first one he brought to the village. In an interview he said that he has a ready-made congregation for any American who might "need a mission."

None of the Pentecostal congregations used as examples in this paper has American personnel attached directly to it. The foreign missionary is a somewhat remote figure at the top of the administrative hierarchy, making only occasional visits to the local conregations, especially in rural areas. Nevertheless, the missionary presence is so pervasive in Haiti that almost all foreigners in rural areas are taken for missionaries. Frequently I was approached by Haitians who thought I was a missionary. Often they proclaimed themselves "fellow" Protestants and would demand gifts of money on that basis. Or they would scold me for stinginess, asking how I could expect people to join my church if I didn't give them anything. Like the founder of the Bethesda Assembly, they assumed that I "needed" a mission and would be willing to pay for it. They also perceived that the mission hierarchy offered one of the few possibilities for well-being, however remote, and wished to attach themselves to it. The Catholic Church quite obviously also has an administrative hierarchy, but the opportunities it offers are much fewer than those offered by the Protestant organizations, which are more widely spread throughout the remote localities of rural Haiti. In fact, the Protestant missionary leader may be the most important non-governmental link to the outside world. Furthermore, licensed Protestant organizations are authorized to administer baptismal certificates and weddings just as the Catholic Church is. Protestantism is associated with development and enlightenment. For many Haitians the Protestant mission represents the wealth of the United States and the acquisition of this wealth is identified with Protestantism.

There may be some tension between the health-oriented and organizational aspects of the Pentecostal mission church. This has already been shown in the schism in the Bethesda Assembly between its local healer-founder and the administrative hierarchy. It can more systematically be seen in the sexual division of labor and opportunity in the Pentecostal mission church. Most of the converts to Pentecostalism in Haiti are women. The principal reason for this is that it is women who are primarily responsible for the health of their families. If a child becomes ill, its mother may convert on account of it. The father may encourage the conversion, but will not often convert himself. Haitians say that men convert less frequently than women because the strictures of Pentecostalism bear more heavily upon them. But it is significant that in the Vodoun system as well women seek treatment through initiation more often than men. Women are active not only as recipients, but also as performers, of Pentecostal health practice. It is usual that the women of a congregation include its most spiritually powerful members, those who have the "gift" of healing and speaking in tongues.

However, administrative authority in Pentecostalism is based not on personal charisma or reputation as a healer, but on a position in the organizational hierarchy. Most of these positions are not available to women. The role of pastor, the highest to which a Haitian can aspire in a Protestant mission, is closed to women. This means that women are all but shut out from the role of broker in relationships with the North American missionary. The roles of translator, clerk and administrator are also usually reserved for men. Even when the foreign mission director is a woman, her assistants are men. A Haitian woman may be an accomplished orator, as all can see in the way she gives "testimony," but she is forbidden to preach. A woman may teach Sunday School lessons (usually to other women or children), but she is not permitted to sit on the local church committee.

The gap between the motivations, roles and styles of women and men in Haitian Pentecostalism became apparent at a fasting service held by some members of the Bethesda Assembly. The service was held in the home of one of the women in the congregation. All but three of the participants were women. All of the women sat on mats on the dirt floor, sang rhythmic Creole songs, spoke "in tongues," and prayed over each other. The three men present were the new pastor (the young Bible student), the deacon mentioned earlier, and a former school teacher. The third man was something of a laughing stock in the village. He was wavering in his allegiance between the Bethesda Assembly and another Pentecostal congregation in the hope of being reinstated as a teacher or becoming some kind of assistant to the new pastor. This was the third Protestant group with which he had been affiliated. The three men stood together in a corner of the small room. Their attempts to direct the service seemed drowned in the cacaphony of public prayer and glossolalia which emanated from the women. None of the men sat on the floor with the women. Nor did their shoes join the pile of sandals that the women had made just outside the door of the house.

Conclusions

For Haitian Pentecostals, their new religion emits images of modernization. Pentecostal healing appears to be an effective new means of establishing a relationship with Bon-Dieu and finding relief from illness. In spite of this image, however, Pentecostal healing can be seen as revalidating the traditional belief system. Even though the Pentecostals redefine the loua as evil spirits, they nevertheless reinforce the belief that these spirits exist and are very powerful. Furthermore, Pentecostal healing provides a "last resort" for the traditional healing system, which is based on a distinction between "God-sent" and other illnesses. Even though the Pentecostals must treat all illnesses as if they were "God-sent," they continue to believe in the traditional etiological distinctions.

The conversion of an individual is regarded as a personal rather than a family matter. Hence, conversion to Protestantism does not interfere with the cult of the loua on the part of the convert's kin. In fact, devoutedly Vodounist kin may encourage the conversion of a sick family member. In sum, the healing aspect of Pentecostalism tends to validate the belief system of Vodoun even if Pentecostals denigrate the rituals and specialists associated with that system. In this respect, Pentecostalism represents an innovation within the traditional belief system rather than a restructuring of it.

The Protestant hierarchical structure is without doubt an important new element in Haitian society, with the potential of becoming an even more significant means of integration on the local, regional and national levels. However, the hierarchical aspect of Pentecostalism channels Haitian aspirations into directions which increase a sense of dependency and inferiority.

It is striking that the non-hierarchical relationships among fellow Pentecostals are not often mobilized outside of the narrow aims of church activities. Fellow congregants do not join each other in the fields or in the marketplace on the basis of their religious affiliation; for example, Pentecostals in rural areas may take a "rejectionist" stance in their rhetoric, but they cannot break off their social relationships with Vodounists. The situation appears to be different in urban areas, however. In some cases at least, rural migrants to the city have replaced kin ties with the fictive kin ties extablished with the "brothers and sisters" in the Pentecostal congregation. This may presage an increased importance for the role of networks established on the basis of congregational membership. If the penetration of foreign capital investment in the small urban industrial sector increases, Pentecostalism may well have a role in the organization and adaptation of the labor force. Already Catholic urban workers are grumbling that Protestant affiliation is an advantage in the Port-au-Prince job market. However, Gerlach is correct in his conclusion that "the economic consequences of being Pentecostal may be ascertained when and if economic opportunities increase generally in Haiti" (1974: 696).

A final image of modernity created by Pentecostalism is the image of an enlightened and generous America. Though this image is tempered by Haitian cynicism, it is widespread. The converse of this image is the devaluation of Haitian culture. Pentecostalism teaches Haitians that they are backward and poor because they are mired in sin. They are told that their sinfulness is rooted in their African origins because they continue the practices of their ancestors in religion and family life. Thus Haiti's poverty vis-à-vis the United States is rationalized on spiritual grounds. One missionary from the United States made this point quite explicitly. He said that Haiti was poor because its people were sinful and that the

United States was rich because of its religious life. A young Haitian convert echoed this view when he proclaimed, "Pèp amérikin sé pèp Bon-Dié mèm!"--"The American People are the real people of God!"

Notes

1. The field research on which this paper is based was conducted from 1974 to 1977. The research was supported by generous grants from the Antilles Research Program, Yale University; The American University; and the National Institute of Mental Health (MH07144-01), for which I wish to express my grateful appreciation. The research was carried out in collaboration with the Centre d'Hygiène Familiale and the Centre de Recherches en Sciences Humaines et Sociales. I wish to thank Katherine Halpern, Ruth Landman, Geoffrey Burkhart, David Rosen, Linda Girdner and David Haines for their useful comments on a draft of this paper.
2. Haitian Creole terms are underlined. If unmarked, they are in a standard HC orthography. If marked (Fr.) they are in French orthography for the convenience of the reader unfamiliar with Haitian Creole. The singular and plural forms of HC nouns are identical.
3. In part the growth of Protestantism in Haiti is due to the struggle of the F. Duvalier government with the Catholic Church, in the course of which North American Protestant missionary activities were permitted and encouraged.

References Cited

Festinger, Leon, Henry W. Riecher and Stanley Schachter
　1964 (orig. 1956) When Prophecy Fails. New York: Harper Torchbooks.

Gerlach. Luther P.
   1974 Pentecostalism: Revolution or Counter-Revolution? In Religious Movements in Contemporary America. Irving I. Zaretsky and Mark P. Leone, eds. Princeton: Princeton University Press.

Gerlach, Luther P. and Virginia H. Hine
   1968 Five Factors Crucial to the Growth and Spread of a Modern Religious Movement. Journal for the Scientific Study of Religion 7: 23-40.

Mintz, Sidney W.
   1966 Introduction to the Second Edition. In The Haitian People. James G. Leyburn. New Haven: Yale University Press.

Murray, Gerald F.
   1977 The Evolution of Haitian Peasant Land Tenure: A Case Study in Agrarian Adaptation to Population Growth. Unpublished Ph.D. Dissertation. Columbia University.

MODERNIZATION AND THE PENTECOSTAL MOVEMENT IN JAMAICA

William Wedenoja
Southwest Missouri State University

In 1962 Jamaica emerged from over 300 years of British colonialism as an independent West Indian nation. It was a society created for the sole purpose of economic exploitation, which forcibly brought many thousands of West Africans to the island as slaves to work sugar plantations. In the process, a system of social stratification based on racial differences and a pluralistic culture of English and West African traditions developed.

By 1800 the plantations were ceasing to prosper and, in 1834, the slaves were emancipated to become free peasants, laborers and artisans. For over a hundred years thereafter, Jamaica struggled unsuccessfully to overcome the legacies of slavery and to develop a new economy, society and culture based on a peasant adaptation. The past thirty years, however, have seen a dramatic modernization, creating great social and cultural changes and grave psychological tensions. This paper deals with the role of religion in that modernization process.

JAMAICAN RELIGION

For about 150 years the Jamaican slave was viewed as property, without a soul to "save." Hence, he was left unchristianized and developed a slave religion based on West African traditions, which were modified to suit the new context. Shortly before the abolition of slavery a variety of charismatic and fundamentalist Protestant churches was allowed to missionize in the island. During the early nineteenth century many black Jamaicans were profoundly affected by these missionaries, but a disenchantment with missionary Christianity eventually led to a number of millenarian and anti-sorcery movements which effected indigenous syncretisms of missionary Christianity and the West African-based slave religion.

Studies of religion in Jamaica and throughout the Caribbean have focused almost exclusively on such syncretistic cults. Hogg (1964), Moore (1953), Simpson (1956) and Barrett (1974, 1977) have provided us with detailed ethnographic accounts of the Pukkumina, Revivalist and Rastafarian syncretistic cults of Jamaica. In other areas of the Caribbean Simpson (1970), Metraux (1972), Herskovits (1937, 1964), Mischel (1958) and Henney (1974), among others, have published accounts of Haitian Vodun, the Shango cult in Trinidad, and the Shakers of St. Vincent.

In 1975 I went to Jamaica to conduct a study of the psychological dynamics of Jamaican cultism, particularly its relations to Jamaican personality. Locating in a rural hamlet in an area known for its proliferation of syncretistic cults, I immediately and unexpectedly discovered a vigorous Pentecostal movement about which nothing had been written. In my hamlet, for example, there were three old and declining Revival cults, four Protestant churches, and two new and vigorous Pentecostal churches. Yet no one had addressed himself to Pentecostalism, which appears to be the fastest growing religious movement in the Caribbean today, and perhaps also in the world.

Calley (1965) has written a detailed study of the social organization of Jamaican Pentecostal and Evangelical sects in England, but it cannot be assumed that the Pentecostalism of emigrants is the same as Pentecostalism in Jamaica. Several scholars have produced very illuminating studies of Pentecostalism in Latin America, such as La Ruffa (1969) for Puerto Rico and Willems (1967) for Brazil, but presumably Pentecostalism has different forms and functions in Latin-Catholic cultures than in the Anglo-Protestant tradition of Jamaica.

The major focus of my fieldwork was syncretistic, Afro-Christian Revival cults, the core religious tradition of the Jamaican masses from 1860 to the Second World War. But Revivalism, I discovered, was being rapidly overtaken and increasingly absorbed by a rampant Pentecostalism. Therefore, although I concentrated my efforts on a study of Revivalism, it seemed essential also to consider Pentecostalism and, indeed, the entire ecology of religion. The concern of this paper is to document this religious change from indigenous cultism to Pentecostalism, identify its causes, and compare the effects of the two religious traditions on Jamaican society and culture. Surely we are dealing with a major cultural change when a society turns from its traditional religion to a new and, in some respects, alien one in so short a period of time. If our functional view is an accurate one, this religious change must have been accompanied by profound social, economic and psychological changes. And, if this is the case, which are the dependent and independent variables?

THE GROWTH OF PENTECOSTALISM

Jamaican Revival cults arose from a redemptive movement, the Great Revival of 1860, in which an institutionalized syncretism was established between missionary Protestantism and the slave religion of African retentions. Revival cults are an ecstatic religion in that they focus on such "manifestations of the Spirit" as possession, trance, omens, prophecy, speaking in tongues, visions and healing. They successfully indigenized Christianity and also brought it under popular control. In many respects, Jamaican Revivalism is strikingly similar to Haitian Vodun, albeit a Protestant version.

In 1907 the Church of God, a newly formed American Pentecostal sect, established a missionary work in Jamaica. Pentecostalism is a Christian sectarian movement of a fundamentalist and salvationist orientation which focuses on religious experience, evidenced characteristically in glossolalia and a conversion experience or "spiritual rebirth." Jesus is its key deity and the New Testament the primary source of doctrine. Pentecostal meetings are often emotionally exciting, with much music, singing, glossolalia, faith healing and the "testimonies" of members. The Church of God had little impact in Jamaica until around the Second World War, when it began its rapid growth, but little is known of the extent of its missionary activity in the early period.

Jamaican Revivalism and Pentecostalism contrast on a number of points. In terms of religious experience, Revivalists permit and encourage a wide range of spiritual behavior while Pentecostalism focuses only on speaking in tongues. Pentecostalism places far greater emphasis on the conversion experience than does Revivalism. God and angels are the key deities of Revivalism while Pentecostalism is Jesucentric. Revivalism concentrates on the Old Testament while Pentecostalism is almost exclusively New Testament in theology. In terms of organization, Revival cults are hierarchical and authoritarian while Pentecostal sects are more congregational.

In 1943 the census recorded 4 percent of the population as Pentecostals.[1] By 1960, 13 percent were identified as Pentecostal and, by 1970, 20 percent were listed as belonging to Pentecostal churches. Unfortunately, because Revival cults are not a recognized sect they have not been enumerated; because of this, Revivalists have traditionally claimed membership in the Church of England or a Baptist denomination.

During the same period that Pentecostalism has grown, the denominations[2] have steadily declined from 82 percent in 1943 to 63 percent in 1960 and 55 percent in 1970 (Department of Statistics 1975).[3] There is, therefore, a striking pattern of decline in denominational Christianity and an accelerating rate of growth in Pentecostalism. At the current rate of growth,

Pentecostal membership should equal denominational membership by about 1990.

Census data are, however, often inaccurate or misleading, and in this case clearly underestimate the rate of religious change. Data from a church survey in the constituency of northern Clarendon, the geographical heart of the Pentecostal movement in Jamaica, reveal that in 1969 45 percent of all church-goers attended Pentecostal churches and 45 percent attended denominational churches (Robotham 1969:60).

In 1976 I undertook a survey of church attendance in a sixty square mile area of northern Manchester parish. Denominational Christianity accounted for 24 percent of all churches and 39 percent of all church-goers, while Pentecostalism accounted for 30 percent of all churches and 25 percent of all church-goers. This survey was undertaken because church attendance statistics seemed to be a more reliable indicator of church popularity than data on church membership or census affiliation. What the study revealed was a much greater decline in denominations and a larger number of Pentecostals than the census data indicate.

So far, statistics on religions other than denominational Christianity and Pentecostalism have been omitted; they are relevant and significant, however. Jamaicans classify churches not so much by theology as by size, either "big" or "small." "Big churches" include the denominations and the Seventh-Day Adventists, which have large buildings and congregations and are seen as "cold" or unemotional, formal, alien, authoritarian and hierarchical.

Religious growth is not strictly in the direction of Pentecostalism; rather, Pentecostalism is part of a larger trend towards "small churches," a close and active fellowship of fervent believers who prefer "emotional" worship and a more popular and democratic organization. The "small churches" include Pentecostals and a variety of Evangelical, non-charismatic sects such as The Church of the First Born and City Mission, as well as the traditional Revival cults. The major difference between Pentecostal and Evangelical churches is that the former permit and encourage greater public demonstration of such "manifestations of the Spirit" as trance, glossolalia and faith healing. Data from my survey of churches in northern Manchester reveal that 50 percent of all churchgoers attend small churches and 50 percent attend big churches. Each church in the survey was also rated on whether or not its attendance was increasing, and this revealed that Pentecostal churches are still growing, but at a slower rate than in previous decades, while Revival cults show a small decline.

My survey of churches also included data on when existing church buildings were established. The majority, 59 percent, were built between 1947 and 1976, indicating a boom in church construction after World War II. Forty percent of these new churches were built between 1947 and 1965, 42 percent between 1957 and 1966, and 18 percent from 1967 to 1976. Thirty-six percent of these new churches are Pentecostal and 83 percent are small churches. Geographically, most of the Pentecostal churches have been established in poorer and more remote communities formerly lacking any church other than a Revival cult. Virtually every remote district in Jamaica now has a Pentecostal church, while Evangelical sects are developing chiefly in the towns.

CAUSES FOR THE GROWTH OF PENTECOSTALISM

Having established that significant religious change is occurring in Jamaica, we now turn to explanations for this change. First, it is important to note that Pentecostalism did not grow immediately after its introduction to the society, but only after Jamaica began to modernize rapidly in the post-war period. Therefore, religion must be our dependent variable.

Pentecostalism has flourished during the period of greatest social change in Jamaica, 1950-1970. This social change is especially significant in that it marked the transition from an agrarian peasant society to an industrializing state. Before the Second World War, Jamaica was a stagnant colonial society ruled by a Crown Colony government intent on developing a predominantly peasant economy. White planters and colonial officials were the controlling elite; mulattoes, Middle Easterners and Chinese dominated the commercial establishment; and a largely disenfranchised and impoverished black and East Indian laboring force and subsistence peasantry constituted the vast majority of the population. These classes were largely endogamous and racially exclusive, and social mobility was insignificant.

The war ushered in many changes: some poor black Jamaicans served overseas in the British army, others worked as temporary farm laborers in the U.S., and several were able to move into positions of greater economic and political power and prestige in the island. From these experiences came a greater knowledge of the developed world, greater assertiveness and confidence, and higher expectations. Economic productivity was stimulated by the war effort as factories were constructed and bauxite production, now the major industry, was initiated. A firm foundation for economic growth and social change was set between 1940-1950.

During the period 1952-1962 Jamaica experienced "one of the highest rates of economic growth in the world" (Tidrick 1973:218), and became committed to transition from a rural peasant society to an urban industrial society. With increasing affluence and social mobility, the rigid system of stratification based on color and inheritance began to erode. Two new classes, a white-collar middle class and an urban proletariat, emerged as significant political forces and became the chief beneficiaries of capital-intensive development. Poor peasants and rural laborers began to acquire the expectations, if not the affluence, of the new classes and some were able to increase their wealth and improve their standard of living, chiefly through the continuation of temporary farm labor employment in the U.S. The growth in membership and influence of labor unions enhanced popular political power and fueled nationalist sentiment. The two dominant labor unions provided secure bases for the development of two national political parties, which led to an increasingly responsive and representative government, nationalistic feeling and, in 1962, political independence.

Modernization, therefore, included techno-economic development, urbanization, increasing affluence and social mobility, a rising standard of living, new expectations for social progress, expansion of the middle class, more democratic politics and materialism. Communities were severely disrupted by modernization due largely to the replacement of subsistence by wage labor: economic achievement replaced personal ties as a basis for prestige, individual effort replaced communal and familial cooperative effort, and division of labor by skill replaced division by age, sex, and kinship. Economic cooperation was replaced by individual competitiveness, which fostered increasing inequality and exchange based on profit rather than sharing. Individual advancement in wealth and prestige undermined traditional patterns of authority in the family and community and migration to urban areas disturbed kin-based relationships. While many saw economic progress in these changes, they also perceived increasing conflict over goods and resources, a challenge to traditional norms, greater personal insecurity and, in general, a rather anomic condition.

These social, economic and political changes also fostered a new sense of self and encouraged new personality traits, the most important being the development of individualism. The wage laborer, striving for personal advancement, cuts himself off significantly from communal obligations and becomes more self-assertive and less submissive and cooperative, acquisitive rather than generous, and self-reliant rather than group-dependent. His drive for personal achievement and mobility leads him to invest his labor and production in what will bring him future personal gain, rather than immediate satisfaction and friendships; he defers self-gratification and denies his labor and production to others. He is future-oriented, self-denying and alone. His inner-directedness involves not only motives or goals but also conscience, as guilt becomes more important than shame.

Such modernization was closely paralleled by the growth of Pentecostalism, and this association does not appear to be coincidental. Pentecostal membership has grown with the GNP and over the same period of rapid growth. It seems reasonable to conclude that economic change is the primary independent variable responsible for the growth of Pentecostalism, although intervening variables such as changes in social structure, personality and values appear to be the direct results of economic change and the proximal causes for religious change. There would also seem to be a feedback effect of religious change reinforcing economic, social and psychological changes. That is, while Pentecostalism arose in response to modernization, it has also taken on the role of reinforcing modernizing trends.

While Pentecostal missionaries from the U.S. and England have played a role in introducing the religion to Jamaica, by far the greatest influence seems to have been repatriated Jamaicans. Since the Second World War Jamaicans have flocked to the U.S. in search of greater economic and educational opportunities. Many come as temporary farm workers for three to six months at a time, while others obtain permanent visas or work illegally with a tourist visa. Like many other immigrant groups, they have been recruited to American Pentecostal sects, which may serve a supportive function in adjusting immigrants to urban life in a new society

(Wilson 1970:71-73). Among the migrants returning to Jamaica, there have been not only Pentecostal converts but also ordained ministers.

The experience, education, wealth and ordination of repatriates elevated their prestige and influence in local communities and enabled them to establish local Pentecostal churches in Jamaica. The returning migrants diffused not only a new faith but also new values and expectations regarding education, economic opportunity, social mobility and political activism. They served as models to emulate and sources of information, leading to a greater public awareness of modern lifestyles and the spread of American values and expectations. Thus, the growth and spread of Jamaican Pentecostalism has been largely an indigenous movement of modernization and Americanization. Affiliation with a Pentecostal sect in Jamaica not only exposes the convert to the values and ideas of modernity and American culture, it is also a symbolic expression of his commitment to a new and changing society. In contrast, Revival cults and denominations are associated with tradition and stasis. Church affiliation is, therefore, an indicator of values and attitudes towards change as well as an ideological force affecting the degree and direction of change.

The association of Pentecostalism with change seems to have been a major factor in its growth over the past two decades, but its spread was also facilitated by traditional modes of religious expression. Jamaican culture is pervasively Christian, fundamentalist and Protestant but this is built upon a West African world view emphasizing group participation, healing, divination, spiritual protection and possession. Before the advent of Pentecostalism it was common for a person to participate in two religious arenas: one maintained membership in a denomination for prestige and the benefits of association with a powerful social institution, but he also participated in ecstatic cultism where greater personal satisfaction was gained. Dual religious affiliation was a reflection of the dual nature of traditional Jamaican culture, more a compartmentalization of English and African cultures than a syncretism.

The introduction of Pentecostalism to Jamaica is not a completely alien innovation; rather, it can be seen as a continuation of traditional Jamaican religion in a new recombination. When a person is attracted to Pentecostalism it may initially serve as a replacement for his Revival cult participation and he will continue to maintain his denominational membership, but after full conversion he will break with his denomination too. Pentecostalism's uniqueness and significance in Jamaican religious evolution is that it offers the appealing features of both denomination and cult; it is a successful syncretism of two opposing religious traditions in Jamaican culture. It has emerged as a religion which is neither foreign like the denominations nor indigenous like the Revival cults, but both indigenous and international. It is a religion for every man regardless of race or class, and it offers both respectable status and popular enthusiasm. Thus it reflects an increasing unification of disparate trends in Jamaican culture, and acts to further the integration of a pluralistic culture and a stratified society.

The social organization of Jamaican Pentecostal sects is also congruent with emerging values of modernity. The colonial government was paternalistic and authoritarian, and this was reflected in the paternalism of denominational ministers and the authoritarianism of Revival cult leaders. Pentecostal sects, on the other hand, are more democratic and egalitarian in organization. Their control is often in the hands of elected officials, and decisions on church issues are made by popular vote. The sects not only reflect these new values, but they also serve to ingrain the democratic process and egalitarian relations in their members.

In addition to these social factors in the spread of Pentecostalism, significant psychological factors are revealed by a comparison of Revivalist and Pentecostal ideology. Revivalists focus on the Old Testament and portray God as a stern, punitive and distant "master" or "father" who has promised collective redemption for His "children" in a future, compensatory "Glory." Followers are to be obedient and submissive, passively conforming to society and accepting its inequities, and coping with common deprivation and oppression by means of a supportive, quasi-familial church. In contrast, Pentecostalism focuses on the New Testament and a Jesus who is more accessible, equal and comforting. Salvation is personal and unmediated, demanding individual effort and responsibility. The status quo is condemned and rejected, and converts look forward to a millenarian revolution in this world. The advent of Pentecostalism, therefore, seems to reflect and encourage psychological changes from communalism to individualism, passivity to activism, submission to assertion, present to future-orientation, immediate to deferred gratification (including self-discipline and self-denial), and shame to guilt--psychological traits associated with modernity.[4]

FUNCTIONS OF PENTECOSTALISM

Pentecostalism developed in Jamaica as a response to modernization, and is an ideological reflection of modern attitudes and values. Moreover, like other social institutions, it serves a number of functions many of which can be seen as cultural adaptations to modernization. The experience and values it offers act to reorient the psyche to better adjust to a new political economy.

Psychologically, Revivalism and Pentecostalism, like most religions, serve to assuage suffering. Revivalism developed in the context of economic deprivation and social oppression. The behavioral environment of Revivalists includes a world plagued by sorcery and malevolent spirits, which act largely as supernatural extensions of human enmity. A basic theme in Revival ceremony is the symbolic expression of repressed hostility: demonic spirits are blamed for illness and misfortune and cultists seek protection from spirits, even attempting to destroy them through ritual exorcism including sword-play. In contemporary Jamaica, however, there has been a breakdown in the social controls preventing the expression of aggression, which is now much more openly expressed than repressed, so the symbolic expression of aggression that Revivalism provided has become less necessary.

The basic theme of the Pentecostal ethos, on the other hand, is identity. Jesus is forcefully cast as an ego ideal—to admire, follow and emulate—until finally, in the spiritual experience of "rebirth," He is internalized as self: to Pentecostals, salvation is becoming like Christ. Pentecostalism can, therefore, be said to provide the convert with a rather immediate and culturally constituted identity reconstruction. This identity is not only personal, in the psychological sense, but also social and cultural. "Being a Christian" involves identification with a social status and group, and bears resemblance to clan or tribal affiliation; it implicitly denies or rejects the statuses of lower-class, black, African, Jamaican or peasant. The society has changed to the extent that traditional social stratification is being eroded and rejected, but it has not yet reached a nationalistic stage wherein people identify as citizens of state; "being a Christian" may then be an intermediate stage in the development of a national identity.

"Being a Christian" and identifying with Christ also provide personal meaning and direction and give one a sense of power and self-esteem. Christ comes to function as a moral role model, replacing traditional norms with Christian ones, and His internalization leads to a greater element of guilt in the conscience. The pressing search for personal identity which is now so noticeable in Caribbean societies is probably rooted in the changes wrought by modernization, although this may be a temporary situation. The citizenry perceive their society as becoming anomic, for old norms are challenged and new ones emerging. Faced with such cultural dissonance, which arouses anxiety and confusion, the convert turns to Pentecostal Christianity, which offers him a clear and dogmatic set of norms and beliefs that apparently resolve his moral crisis. This new certainty of what is good and evil and how one should live not only reduces anxiety and confusion, but also remotivates the individual. Guidelines for action are detailed and new hope is engendered. Such functions are typical of "revitalization movements," whether they be nativistic or millenarian in orientation.

In addition to resolving a mass identity crisis and normative confusion, typical of societies undergoing rapid and major change, Pentecostalism also assuages other pains of modernization. The key means for doing so is the warm personal support the convert receives from his "brethren," who come to act as a fictive family group. Those who are disturbed by the passing of tradition or who may have failed in their attempts at social mobility and achievement find solace, encouragement and cathartic outlets for expressing their frustration, disappointment and anger in Pentecostal services before a concerned and sympathetic audience. In this sense, Pentecostalism functions as a mass form of supportive psychotherapy for casualties of the modernization process.

Pentecostalism encourages the development of psychological traits and patterns of behavior conducive to success in a capitalist economy, including deferral of gratification, thrift and conscientious labor and exchange. Self-denial is a virtue in Pentecostalism, which condemns popular entertainment, fashionable clothes, jewelry and other forms of conspicuous consumption. Self-discipline is enforced by a stringent moral code which prohibits such behaviors as promiscuity, illegitimacy, concubinage, drunkeness, violence and religious "backsliding." Achievement motivation is nurtured by competition for election to church offices and even, perhaps, in striving to achieve "spiritual baptism" by the Holy Ghost.

Pentecostalism has also come to play important roles in the social system. In many Jamaican communities Pentecostal churches are the only group beyond the family, and they act as community centers in providing leadership, entertainment, and a forum for the expression and formulation of public opinion, sponsoring local events and serving as agencies for social control and social welfare.

Pentecostalism is a subtle revolution that induces a great number of social, cultural and psychological changes. But it also has the potential to become a revolutionary political force. Its this-worldly theology rejects the status quo and preaches that a millenial revolution will elevate Pentecostals above the "ungodly"--the large land-owners, businessmen and politicians. It creates fervent believers who are linked in an island-wide network that cannot be undermined or suppressed. Perhaps most importantly, its leadership and control are popular, or in the hands of the ordinary man. It is fundamentally a grass-roots populist movement, in contrast to the past and present domination of society and politics by the elite and middle-class minorities. Jamaican Pentecostalism can become a potent force for greater popular democracy. It has the organization and membership to elect popular leaders who are responsive to their needs, which can free the political system from the hands of a privileged and remote oligarchy.

Finally, Pentecostalism seems to be an effective vehicle for the further integration of a stratified and pluralistic society and culture. It has been successful in gathering converts from all sectors of the lower and middle class and from a number of racial groups, unlike previous religions in Jamaica. In order to remain competitive, Revival cults and denominational churches are becoming increasingly Pentecostal in their ritual and ideology. Soon, regardless of church, the dominant Jamaican religious ethos will be Pentecostal, and this may be the beginning of a unified culture with a common, rather than pluralistic, value structure and world view.

THE PENTECOSTAL REVOLUTION

My analysis has revealed Pentecostalism to be a dynamic and adaptive, even revolutionary, force in modern Jamaica. It is an important expression of, and force for, social, cultural and psychological modernization, although its causes, functions and effects will differ from society to society. Many, however, regard it as a conservative, even reactionary force. Indeed, Pentecostalism in the Third World is often accused of being a form of American cultural imperialism which only serves to protect American interests and encourage capitalistic sentiments. This has not been a concern in my analysis of the growth and effects of Pentecostalism, and I raise it now only because it is an issue fraught with biases and misunderstandings.

Pentecostalism is a subtle but profound revolution because it is low-key, religious and not obviously political. It should not be compared to the American, French, Russian or Mexican revolutions but to the rise of Christianity and the Reformation. It is an ideological concomitant to modernization, which can be compared to the agricultural and industrial revolutions. As Gerlach and Hine (1970:xii) have noted, "each of these radical changes involved new forms of religious thought and new concepts of the relationship between man and man." Pentecostalism is a revolutionary faith because it effects changes in self and the relations between self and others, which incidentally also affects the established churches, and generates an ideological force promoting corresponding changes in society, economy and polity.

Pentecostalism is not merely the conversion of Jamaicans to an American faith. It flourishes in Jamaica because it has been indigenized by Jamaicans, modified according to the Jamaican religious tradition, at the same time that it introduces new ideological elements conducive to modernization.

Jamaican Pentecostalism is not a missionary church. Its churches are fiercely independent, they were initiated by Jamaicans, and they are controlled by Jamaicans. While the origin of the movement may be in America, its Jamaican form is a genuine expression of emerging Jamaican needs, values and sentiments. Its dogma does spread and reinforce values and behaviors conducive to modernization, capitalism and democracy but this reflects, and is adaptive to, current social and economic trends.

There are many in Jamaica who oppose Pentecostalism, and they are largely people in positions of power; the traditional elite in government, politics, business and religion. Pentecostalism is seen as a threat by the denominations, misguided belief by the better-off, and a nuisance to the government. This is a clear sign that Pentecostalism is revolutionary; as Gerlach and Hine (1970:xiii) note: "change may be defined as radical if those who occupy positions of power in the existing social structure resist that change." Pentecostalism may be, in part, an "opiate of the masses" but, as Americans discovered in the sixties, opiates may anaesthetize in the short run but also induce enduring changes in self, patterns of relations, values and ideas.

Jamaican Pentecostalism continues in the Jamaican historical tradition of slave revolts, African cults and separatist sects in mobilizing and uniting the deprived, neglected, powerless and oppressed so that their needs and desires can be heard and implemented. In Jamaican culture, the revolutionist response has been more often garbed in religion than in politics, and religious movements have proven to be more persistent and enduring than political ones.

Pentecostalism is not the only revolutionary faith in modern Jamaica. The cult of Rastafarism has grown during the same period of time, although it has a nativistic orientation. Rastafarism, which worships Haile Selassie as god and includes meditation and the smoking of marijuana in its rituals, reflects some aspects of modernization too in that it stresses individualism and egalitarianism. It is more obviously revolutionary because of its extreme rejection of, and withdrawal from, society and because it has taken political positions. However, it is largely a movement of the lumpenproletariat: chronically unemployed, black, urban, male youth who are victims of modernization and therefore seek a third alternative. While the movement has been very influential in heightening social consciousness and creating a new pride in African and Jamaican indigenous culture, it does not have the widespread appeal of Pentecostalism and does not extensively cut across racial, class, cultural and age barriers. Its lasting influence on the religion of Jamaica will probably be a further indigenization of Jamaican Pentecostalism.

While it is worthwhile to consider the effects of Western Christendom on Third World societies, we also need to ponder how the embracement and indigenization of Christianity by Third World societies will affect Western Christendom. Culture contact transforms both parties, colonizer and colonized, although we usually focus only on transformation of the colonized. Third World Christianities may promote a new form of Christendom as we enter into the era of a global culture.

NOTES

Acknowledgements. This paper was originally, in a shorter version, prepared for reading in a symposium on "Pentecostalism and Modernization" at the annual meeting of the American Anthropological Association in Houston, Texas on November 30, 1977. I am grateful for the critical reading of various drafts by Professors Melford E. Spiro, Lloyd R. Young and Ravindra G. Amonker.

The research on which this paper is based was supported by an NIMH predoctoral traineeship and a fellowship from the Organization of American States, and resulted in my doctoral dissertation "Religion and Adaptation in Rural Jamaica" accepted by the Department of Anthropology of the University of California, San Diego in 1978.

[1] Pentecostalism has been particularly prone to schisms and there are a plethora of Pentecostal sects in Jamaica, some international and some national; they include "Apostolic" churches such as the Apostolic Church of God, Church of Jesus Christ Apostolic and Shiloah Apostolic Church and the "Churches of God" such as the Pentecostal Church of God, New Testament Church of God, Church of God in Christ, Church of God of Prophecy and the Four Square Church of God.

[2] Churches classified as denominations include the Roman Catholics, Church of England, Presbyterian, Moravian, Congregationalist, Methodist and Baptist churches.

[3] Statistics for 1970 religious affiliation were compiled from unpublished data generously made available by the Department of Statistics of Jamaica.

[4] I have contrasted Revivalism and Pentecostalism as ideal types. Currently, it is not so easy to distinguish them because Revivalism and the denominations are incorporating Pentecostal ideas

and practices in an attempt to remain competitive.
For example, a Church of England in my research
area initiated healing by laying on of hands,
altar calls, glossolalia and total immersion
adult Baptism during my stay. A Presbyterian
church adopted regular testimonies and permitted
glossolalia. It also initiated Sunday night
evangelistic rallies and invited Pentecostal
leaders to preach.

REFERENCES CITED

Barrett, Leonard E.
  1974 Soul Force: African Heritage in Afro-American Religion. Garden City, New York: Doubleday.

  1977 The Rastafarians: Sounds of Cultural Dissonance. Boston: Beacon.

Calley, Malcolm
  1965 God's People: West Indian Pentecostal Sects in England. London: Oxford University Press.

Department of Statistics
  1975 Statistical Yearbook of Jamaica, 1974. Kingston.

Gerlach, Luther P. and Virginia H. Hine
  1970 People, Power, Change: Movements of Social Transformation. Indianapolis: Bobbs-Merrill.

Henney, Jeanette H.
  1974 Spirit Possession Belief and Trance Behavior in Two Fundamentalist Groups in St. Vincent. *In* Trance, Healing, and Hallucination: Three Field Studies in Religious Experience, Felicitas D. Goodman, Jeannette H. Henney and Esther Pressel, pp. 1-111. New York: John Wiley.

Herskovits, Melville J.
  1937 Life in a Haitian Valley. New York: Knopf.

Herskovits, Melville J. and Frances S.
  1964 Trinidad Village. New York: Octagon.

Hogg, Donald W.
  1964 Jamaican Religions: A Study in Variations. Ph.D. dissertation, Department of Anthropology, Yale University.

La Ruffa, Anthony L.
  1969 Culture Change and Pentecostalism in Puerto Rico. Social and Economic Studies 18:273-281.

Metraux, Alfred
  1972 Voodoo in Haiti. New York: Schocken.

Mischel, Frances O.
  1958 A Shango Group and the Problem of Prestige in Trinidad Society. Ph.D. dissertation, Department of Anthropology, Ohio State University.

Moore, Joseph G.
  1953 Religion of Jamaican Negroes: A Study of Afro-American Acculturation. Ph.D. dissertation, Department of Anthropology, Northwestern University.

Robotham, Hugh
  1969 North Clarendon Rural Development (Self Help) Project Survey. Kingston: Jamaica Agricultural Society.

Simpson, George E.
  1956 Jamaican Revivalist Cults. Social and Economic Studies 5:321-414.

  1970 Religious Cults of the Caribbean: Trinidad, Jamaica, and Haiti. Rio Piedras: University of Puerto Rico Press.

Tidrick, Gene
  1973 Some Aspects of Jamaican Emigration to the United Kingdom 1953-1962. Reprinted <u>in</u> Work and Family Life: West Indian Perspectives, Lambros Comitas and David Lowenthal, eds., pp. 189-219. Garden City, New York: Doubleday.

Willems, Emilio
  1967 Followers of the New Faith: Culture Change and the Rise of Protestantism in Brazil and Chile. Nashville: Vendervilt University Press.

Wilson, Bryan
  1970 Religious Sects. New York: McGraw-Hill.

PENTECOSTALISM IN PUERTO RICAN SOCIETY
Anthony L. LaRuffa
Herbert H. Lehman College, CUNY

The general purpose of this paper is to discuss some of the characteristics and consequences of the Pentecostal movement in Puerto Rican society. More specifically, I shall consider some historical and descriptive data on Pentecostalism within two contexts; the island and the community of San Cipriano.[1] This will be followed by an interpretation of the role of Pentecostalism within the community and in Puerto Rican society as a whole.

THE HISTORICAL CONTEXT

Pentecostalism as a religious movement may be identified in terms of seven characteristics: a fundamentalist interpretation of the Bible; conversion as a crisis experience which initiates a sinner into a life of holiness; a belief in the second coming of Christ; an emphasis on faith healing; baptism by total immersion; expressive participation in religious services; and an active seeking of possession by the Holy Spirit, which is manifested by speaking in tongues. It is this last characteristic which distinguishes Pentecostalism from a number of similar religious movements including, among others, the Holiness movement of the nineteenth and twentieth centuries, the earlier Wesleyan movement, and a number of present-day Baptist denominations. While such movements recognize and accept possession by the Holy Spirit, Pentecostals actively seek this type of religious experience. Recently, a Pentecostal-like phenomenon has affected a number of traditional religious bodies. Episcopalian, Presbyterian and Catholic communicants, to name some, have formed

...ial groupings, the membership of which has ...n seriously committed to a Holy Spirit possession experience. These are not Pentecostal churches but, rather, sectarian bodies incorporating a Pentecostal characteristic, albeit an important one.

Two centuries of American revivalism provided a matrix for the growth of Pentecostalism during the first decade of the twentieth century. Although aspects of the movement appeared to be linked up with various fundamentalist sects, a crystallization of traits and a proselytizing momentum took form in southern California in the early years of this century. It was from this area, especially the Los Angeles region, that many of the convert-seekers carried the "word" to different parts of the country and across the seas.

Data on the early development of Pentecostalism in Puerto Rico is sparse. A number of Pentecostal ministers have indicated to me that a few churches were established there between 1910 and 1930. According to my informants, the movement expanded impressively during the 1930s when Puerto Rico, like so many other areas, was afflicted by a devastating economic depression.

More conclusive information is available for the forties and subsequent years. Comparing Pentecostal organizations of the early forties with other Protestant churches, Davis (1942: 14-15) ranks them first in the number of churches, sixth in the number of constituents, first in the number of candidates for baptism, and first in the number of pastors. Davis' data indicate that Pentecostals comprised 8.5 per cent of the Protestants in Puerto Rico at that time (ibid.).

Ten years later the number of Pentecostals increased to 34,100, or 25 per cent of the total Protestant communicants (Bingle and Grubb 1952: 246). The World Christian Handbook 1962 figures place the Pentecostal population at 40,352, roughly 23 per cent of the total number of Protestants (Coxhill and Grubb 1962:124-125). Later figures indicate that more than 53,000 Puerto Ricans claimed membership in Pentecostal churches; that is, approximately 25 per cent of the island Protestants were Pentecostals.

The figures from the <u>World Christian Handbook</u> underestimate the Pentecostal population of Puerto Rico since only three or four church bodies are listed. A more accurate, and yet fairly conservative, estimate of the Pentecostal population in Puerto Rico in the mid-sixties is approximately 70,000-80,000. Recent figures indicate that Puerto Rico's Pentecostal population is currently about 225,000 (<u>New York Times</u>, June 10, 1979:43).

PENTECOSTALISM IN SAN CIPRIANO

Pentecostal proselytizing had some success in and around San Cipriano during the mid-thirties. A native Ciprianera who had converted to Pentecostalism at the Bethel Pentecostal Church in "El Barrio" (New York City) returned to the community to mount an aggressive evangelical campaign and help organize the first church. Later, a number of her disciples broke with her and engaged in independent proselytizing efforts. Some then went on to establish their own churches and, subsequently, played important roles in the expansion of the movement. The first church was founded in Barriada Toledo with just a small number of communicants. Membership increased to just over one hundred at the time of my field research.[2] By the end of the 1930s, a second Pentecostal church was established just off the main road at the western end of San Cipriano. Between 1939 and 1949 the church remained relatively static with membership rarely exceeding thirty-five. In 1949, however, a young, charismatic minister took charge of the church and membership increased steadily. By the mid-sixties, the Christian Missionary Church was

tedly the largest Pentecostal church in
ommunity with 140 members. By the late
, a third church was organized, and by
, the membership included approximately
eighty people.

In the early fifties, a "campo" (door-to-door proselytizing campaign) was organized in Barriada Miñi Miñi, culminating, shortly thereafter, in the construction of yet another Pentecostal church, the Church of God (Cleveland, Tennessee).

During the early years of the 1960s, two new churches were constructed and two "campos" inaugurated in San Cipriano. Table 1 summarizes the membership data of the various Pentecostal churches and "campos" in the community as of 1964.

A brief review of statistical information available for Protestants in general, and Pentecostals in particular, reveals some interesting problems. The number of Pentecostals in San Cipriano accounts for nearly 80 per cent of the total Protestant population of the community. This proportion is considerably higher than the proportion of Pentecostals (27 per cent-30 per cent) among the Puerto Rican Protestant population. The total number of Protestants, including Baptists, Adventists, Prophetics, and Pentecostals, reflects, to a great extent, the proportion for all of Puerto Rico, about 13 per cent.[3] The situation in San Cipriano, however, cannot be viewed as typical for all of Puerto Rico, nor for that matter, any one specific region of the island. It does, nevertheless, provide us with a context for an interpretive analysis of the content and consequences of a relatively successful religious movement.

THE MIÑI MIÑI CHURCH OF GOD

In many ways the Miñi Miñi Church of God is fairly representative of the Pentecostal bodies in San Cipriano. Whether one selects the social composition of the memberships, local church organizational features, or dogma and ritual, the similarities with the other Pentecostal churches are remarkable. I concentrated on the Church of God because the congregation was small enough for me to get to know all the members well. Furthermore, I had the opportunity to observe a "campo" in my own neighborhood. To broaden my perspective, however, I periodically visited the other Pentecostal churches in San Cipriano, as well as some churches outside the community, and interviewed officials and communicants.

In order to better understand why "campo" activities were initiated in the "barriada" (Miñi Miñi), it is necessary to consider how certain personalities and events created the circumstances which, ultimately, led to the construction of the Church of God.

At the time of my research, Felipe[4] and his wife, Engracia, were the dominant figures in the Miñi Miñi Church, positions they had maintained since the church's inception. After converting to Pentecostalism in 1948 at age twenty-four, Felipe began attending services regularly at New Jerusalem (Assembly of Christian Churches) in Barriada Melilla. It was at this time that he met Engracia, an exceedingly devout woman and one of the founders of the Melilla church. They were married in 1949. Soon after the marriage, Felipe and Engracia requested support from the Assembly of Christian Churches to undertake "campo" activities in Barriada Miñi Miñi, the people of which, they believed to be in desperate need of salvation. Their goal was to build a church there. Felipe's prospects in the Melilla church were somewhat limited. He could expect a deaconry or, if fortunate enough, an assistant pastorate. The elderly pastor had firm control over his flock and he was surely not about to relinquish power to an ambitious young man. Nor was Felipe patient enough to wait for the man's resignation or demise. Moreover, Engracia, a forceful and active woman, had to accept a subordinate role in the office of the missionary. The pastor's wife had the advantage of her husband's position in establishing herself as the ranking female in the congregation. It was inevitable that Felipe and Engracia would strike out on their own.

Their request for support from the Assembly of Christian Churches (U. S.-based Pentecostal organization) was refused. Instead they were offered an opportunity to proselytize in the Dominican Republic. They declined. Both Felipe and Engracia felt strongly about remaining in San Cipriano and organizing a "campo" in Miñi Miñi, the "barriada" in which Felipe was born and raised. The couple soon left the Assembly of Christian Churches and sought the assistance of the Church of God. The latter church body agreed and within three years "The Church of God (Mission Board) of Miñi Miñi" was built just a few yards from the home of Felipe and Engracia.

From 1952 to 1958, Felipe, Engracia, and the latter's brother-in-law, Joaquin, labored to bring new members into the church. Felipe utilized his kinship network to attract converts, and, consequently, a number of the congregation were his kinspeople. Felipe resigned his pastorate in 1958 but continued to maintain a strong hold over the church.

In 1961, Joaquin, Engracia's brother-in-law, became the third pastor of the Miñi Miñi Church of God following the resignation of a missionary student who had assumed the position on a temporary basis. During this time, Felipe became active in the district affairs of the Church of God, an involvement which provided him with considerable local power and served as a springboard for a more lucrative and prestigious position in a suburb of Caguas. Joaquin, while, continued as pastor for about six ye before resigning. Once again a student missionary was assigned to lead the congreg

The Congregation

In the mid-sixties the Miñi Miñi Church of God book membership was forty-two, of which twenty-three were children. Of the nineteen adult members (seven men and twelve women) about twelve attended three or more services per week. Although there were five more women than men, the majority of men consistently attended more services than many of the women, and from time to time the adult males outnumbered the adult females. Comparative figures on attendance from other Pentecostal churches in the community suggested that the man:woman attendance ratio was not nearly as close but, nevertheless, indicated a strong commitment by men to Pentecostal activities. My records of Catholic services, for example, showed a man:woman ratio of 1:3 compared to 1:2 or less at Pentecostal services.

Selected Socio-Economic Data on Members

Membership in the Miñi Miñi Church of God was drawn from fifteen households, and in only eight of the fifteen households were all adult members Pentecostals. The other seven were mixed households in that one or more of the adult members belonged to other religious organizations. These seven households were categorized as Pentecostal-Catholic.

Information on income indicated that two of the households showed an income of better than $2,000. The remaining thirteen earned less than $2,000.

Data on house types further corroborated the impoverishment of most of the households. Nearly two-thirds of the dwellings were small, wooden and, in most cases, substandard. This means that nearly 69 per cent of the membership lived in overcrowded conditions, given the fact that average household size was computed to be 5.6.

Some comparative information on a Church of God "campo" in another "barriada" of San Cipriano suggested that Pentecostal converts were not exclusively drawn from the most destitute sector of the population. The income distribution of one-third of those households fell between $2,000 and $5,000, a situation which I had judged to be lower middle class in terms of a local social class profile. None of the Pentecostal or part-Pentecostal households exceeded the $2,000-$5,000 income distribution. Similarly, more of the Las Carreras "Campo" membership lived in more spacious and somewhat better constructed houses. Despite the campo" figures, my general impression of Pentecostal church members throughout the community was that their living conditions could be characterized as ranging from very poor to moderately poor.

Tables 2 and 3 list the adult membership by name, age, education, marital status, and occupation for the Miñi Miñi Church of God and the Las Carreras "Campo."

INTERPRETATION

Pentecostalism as a religious movement showed a mild growth spurt during the 1930s but experienced a marked expansion in the post-World War II era. Not surprisingly, this paralleled a stabilization, at least for the time, of Puerto Rico's political status. Primarily, through the efforts of Munoz Marin, a commonwealth association was negotiated with the U. S. government with statehood as an unlikely alternative, and independence as a distinctly remote possibility. It would seem that for many Puerto Ricans the 1950s and 1960s promised unprecedented economic growth with hundreds of millions of dollars pouring in from shrewd U. S. investors who capitalized on the liberal tax laws and plentiful, cheap labor. Industrial plants began appearing in many parts of the island, especially in and around the larger cities. Suburbs became commonplace. In a number of areas interlocking city-suburban networks formed sprawling conurbations, some of which extended for miles along the northeastern and south-central coastal regions. Comfortable looking homes and expensive U. S.-made cars were constant reminders of a new affluence buttressed by heavy consumer borrowing. Television mesmerized the viewers with flashy symbols of modern-day living. Puerto Ricans developed into consumers par excellence, ready recipients of large quantities of U. S. produce.

It was within this general socio-cultural context that the Pentecostal movement experienced a modicum of success. It would be useful to discuss some of the probable reasons for its expansion in the fifties and sixties with particular emphasis on its role in the community of San Cipriano.

One could begin with a question: Why did some Ciprianeros convert, while others did not? A thorough answer requires considerably more socio-psychological data than I now possess. Moreover, since so many variables are involved, a number of which I was totally unaware of at the time of my research and some of which I am still uncertain about, I intend to limit myself to certain specific factors which I feel are relevant in understanding the modest success of the movement in the community.

The most pervasive and overriding factor in the lives of the Ciprianeros was poverty and, in so many cases, hopeless poverty. Yet, for some, the flickering of affluence provided a faint glimmer of hope. Very few, however, were able to enjoy a style of comfort. Four categories, the destitute, the hopeful poor, the moderately comfortable, and the comfortable, could be viewed as the local class strata in that the

chances of these groupings were reflected in
incomes earned by household members.
viduals and families assessed themselves
in terms of other individuals and other families:
<u>a cane worker earned $600 a year, a factory
worker made three times as much</u>. A spacious
cement house with two bedrooms, an indoor bath,
and a car port, all owned by a local teacher and
his small family, dwarfed a shabby, two-room
wooden structure that housed an underemployed
construction laborer, his wife, and six children.
These patent variations in life styles were,
often enough, experienced by members of the same
kindred. Status and the material comforts of
life were scarce resources in an impoverished
community. And yet, the consequences of a
massive industrialization program, many of
which had local and regional repercussions
exacerbated the conditions of poverty in San
Cipriano by generating a more affluent and
considerably smaller middle sector.

How did one take the measure of oneself and
others in such a context? How did one cope with
gnawing poverty when one's neighbor or kinsperson
ate better, dressed more stylishly, and luxu-
riated under a warm indoor shower? For some
Ciprianeros membership in the Pentecostal church
was a way of coping with the pressures of life.
The demonstrative rituals acted as forms for a
collective catharsis; prayers were recitations
of hope, entreaty, and gratitude for health and
a better paying job; and the comraderie of the
communicants whose life chances were more or less
similar was supportive for the indivdual and was
expressed in emotional and material ways.

For the very few, <u>Pentecostalism became a
vehicle for social and economic mobility</u>.
Felipe and his wife, Engracia, were the most
affluent members of the Mini Mini Church of God
Although Felipe's income was not derived from
church-related activities, his status in the
local church and his office as district pastor
enabled him to exploit a network of potential

customers for his appliance business. In
addition, his contacts with the Puerto Rican
hierarchy of the Church of God proved advanta-
gious since he was ultimately given a pastor-
ship in a middle-class suburb of Caguas where
his proselytizing and salesmanship undoubtedly
yielded greater returns.

There were, also, those Pentecostal evangelists who basked in the limelight of fame and
comfort. Two of them passed through San
Cipriano during my stay in the community: one,
a defrocked Catholic priest from Colombia, S. A.,
converted to Pentecostalism and became a popular
preacher in the South America and Caribbean
areas; the other was one of Puerto Rico's most
celebrated evangelists and a popular radio
personality among Pentecostals and other funda-
mentalists. Huge crowds attended both events
which proved to be, among other things, fund-
raising affairs.

The Puerto Rican evangelist was, far and
away, the more successful of the two. During his
three-day revival in the community, he preached
to large audiences. Throughout the period he
pleaded for contributions. It was on the last
evening, however, that he outdid himself.
Frequently during the services he badgered the
people for more money as his assistants
skittered about with collection containers
which appeared to be considerably larger than
the ones used the previous two evenings. The
people responded generously and the evangelist,
with his entourage, left San Cipriano spiritually uplifted and somewhat wealthier.

In assessing some of the consequences of
Pentecostalism in the community of San Cipriano,
one could make some guarded generalizations about
the broader societal context. Moreover, my own
experiences with, and information about
Pentecostals in other parts of the island seem
to substantiate my impressions.

One of the most striking aspects of Pentecostalism, like a number of similar fundamentalist movements of the past, is its accommodating propensity, i.e., its adaptability to changing socio-cultural conditions. Although beginning as a religion of the poor and oppressed and certainly continuing as such for many Ciprianeros and other Puerto Ricans, it readily adjusted itself to more affluent conditions. Some Pentecostal churches in Puerto Rico, for example, have a constituency which is part professional and fits into the middle and upper-middle sectors of the population. These churches have taken on many of the staid characteristics of the more traditional Protestant denominations.

This accommodating feature of Pentecostalism, at least in the context of Puerto Rican society, make it supportive of the existing socio-economic and political conditions. During my stay in Puerto Rico not one Pentecostal argued for independence as a desirable political alternative. All those I spoke with upheld the commonwealth status or suggested statehood as the only alternative. Independence, according to my Pentecostal informants, would lead, inevitably, to a communist takeover and another Cuban state in the Caribbean.

Since Puerto Rico's political and economic conditions have been determined primarily by its relationship to the United States, an accommodating movement such as Pentecostalism, tends to reinforce an Americanization process which, in the past three decades, has turned Puerto Rico into an ideological, economic, and political satellite of the United States.

Table 1 Pentecostal Churches and "Campos" in San Cipriano: location and membership

Pentecostal Church or "Campo"	Location	Total membership
Assembly of Christian Churches	Toledo	102
Assembly of Christian Churches	Melilla	80
Christian Missionary	Western Extremity of San Cipriano	140
Christian Missionary "Campo"	Vieques	13
Church of God (Cleveland, Tenn.)	Miñi Miñi	42
Church of God (Cleveland, Tenn.) "Campo"	Las Carreras	94
"Lirios del Valle"	Vieques	15
"Voz en el Desierto"	Miñi Miñi	37
Total		523

NOTE: From San Cipriano: Life in a Puerto Rican Community, Anthony L. LaRuffa (New York: Gordon and Breach, Science Publishers, Inc., 1971). p. 89

Table 2. Miñi Miñi Church of God adult membership: name, age, education, marital status, and occupation

Name	Age	Education (Years)	Marital status	Occupation
Males				
Adolfo	52	4	Married	Cane Picker
Augusta	34	12	Single	Unemployed
Cecilio	65	0	Married	Foreman
Enrique	30	9	Married	Construction
Felipe	38	12	Married	Salesman
Joaquin	42	8	Married	Cane Picker
Marcelo	30	8	Single	Cane Picker
Females				
Camila	28	7	Widow	Housewife
Carmen	35	9	Married	Housewife
Elena	44	2	Married	Housewife
Engracia	38	8	Married	Housewife
Eufemia	55	7	Widow	Housewife
Eugenia	35	3	Married	Housewife
Isabel	42	2	Married	Housewife
Juana	75	3	Widow	Housewife
Luisa	29	9	Married	Housewife
María	50	7	Widow	Housewife
Nicolasa	50	2	Widow	Housewife
Rosa	29	10	Married	Housewife

NOTE: From San Cipriano: Life in a Puerto Rican Community, Anthony L. LaRuffa (New York: Gordon and Breach, Science Publishers, Inc., 1971). p. 101

Table 3 Las Carreras "Campo" adult membership: name, age, education, marital status, and occupation

Name	Age	Education (Years)	Marital status	Occupation
Males				
Arturo	49	4	Widower	Unemployed
Diego	36	—	Married	Cane picker/migrant worker
Ignacio	38	12+	Married	Electrician
Jesús	41	3	Married	Cane picker
Miguel	47	7	Married	Janitor
Females				
Barbara	36	7	Married	Housewife
Beatriz	34	7	Married	Housewife
Dolores	34	8	Married	Housewife
Elisa	47	8	Married	Housewife
Ines	38	8	Married	Housewife
Josefina	48	5	Married	Housewife
Margarita	43	8	Married	Housewife
Maria	27	11	Married	Housewife
María	68	—	Widow	Housewife
Rosario	55	3	Married	Housewife
Sara	45	5	Widow	Housewife

NOTE: From *San Cipriano: Life in a Puerto Rican Community*, Anthony L. LaRuffa (New York, Gordon and Breach, Science Publishers, Inc., 1971). p. 110

NOTES

[1] San Cipriano is a fictive name for the "barrio" in which I did my field work during the mid-1960s. Most of the data presented in this paper reflect my field experiences at that particular time period. For a more complete description and interpretation of those experiences see *Pentecostalism in a Puerto Rican Community* (1966) and *San Cipriano: Life in a Puerto Rican Community* (1972).

[2] These figures and those that follow include all members, both baptized and unbaptized. The final figures reflect church membership in 1964.

[3] Although the community and island figures for Protestant membership are very similar, this does not necessarily imply that the same denominations are represented, nor that the proportion for each denomination is comparable.

[4] In 1967 Felipe and Engracia left San Cipriano to take up pastoral duties in a larger and more middle-class-oriented Church of God church in Caguas, a city situated about eighteen miles south of San Juan.

REFERENCES CITED

Bingle, E. J., and K. Grubb (Eds.).
  1952 World Christian Handbook. London:
    Dominion Press.
Coxhill, H. W., and K. Grubb (Eds.)
  1962 World Christian Handbook. London:
    Dominion Press.
  1968 World Christian Handbook. London:
    Dominion Press.
Davis, J. Merle
  1942 The Church in Puerto Rico's Dilemma.
    New York: International Missionary Council.
LaRuffa, Anthony L.
  1966 Pentecostalism in a Puerto Rican
    Community. Unpublished Ph.D. dissertation,
    Columbia University, New York
  1972 San Cipriano: Life in a Puerto Rican
    Community. New York: Gordon and Breach,
    Science Publishers, Inc.
New York Times
  June 10, 1979, p. 43.

PENTECOSTAL EXORCISM AND MODERNIZATION IN TRINIDAD, WEST INDIES

Stephen D. Glazier

University of Connecticut

The relationship between church growth and modernization[1] is a very tenuous one which has occupied the attention of sociologists and anthropologists of religion for well over fifty years. It was demonstrated time and again that a church may play a profound modernizing role without substantial growth and vice versa.

In my study of Pentecostalism in Trinidad[2], I discovered that these two variables are related, albeit indirectly, i.e., the appeal and subsequent 'growth' of Pentecostalism may be attributed partially to its handling of traditional, and decidedly unmodern, beliefs concerning Obeah and demon possession. The church has developed a very modern way of dealing with these beliefs which may, in turn, have an unexpected modernizing influence on the life of the individual.

Less than fifteen miles off the coast of Venezuela, Trinidad is an island of astonishing complexity. Its slightly over one million inhabitants reflect a series of migrations which resulted in the displacement of the aboriginal population and their replacement by slaves and indentured servants of African, Chinese and Indian origin. Today, few aboriginals remain. According to a recent census,[3] the population is roughly 40% Black and 40% East Indian with the remainder classified as White, Chinese or Syrian.

Racial diversity on the island makes for a complicated system of social and economic stratification. Commerce and industry are dominated by Whites, Chinese and East Indians, while Blacks tend to dominate in political matters. This has given rise to considerable friction between Trinidad's various racial and/or ethnic groups.

The religious life of the island is also complex. Introduced by the Spanish in the 16th Century, the Roman Catholic Church has remained viable and Protestantism exerted a tremendous influence due to missionary activity in the 1800's (Simpson, 1976). Considerable religious syncretism has taken place between religions of African and European origin and much of the literature on Trinidad's religions has focused on the various cult groups which are products of this "syncretism" (Herskovits and Herskovits, 1947: Mischel, 1957; Simpson, 1970, 1978; Pollak-Eltz, 1970).

On the basis of outward appearance, the growth of the Pentecostal Church has been phenomenal. In 1960, there were fewer than four thousand members of the Pentecostal Church in Trinidad.[4] By 1970, thousands of people attended individual congregations and Pentecostalism had spread to every community on the island, with some communities claiming more than one church. I would estimate that over twenty thousand people participate in Pentecostal services each week.

The overall trend has been toward larger churches. The church at Curepe, for example, was dedicated in 1961; by 1971, an addition to the church was completed doubling its size. By 1973, the church had again outgrown its facilities and another addition was built. In 1976, when I began my fieldwork, the church was able to seat approximately twelve hundred; in 1978, there were another eight hundred seats with plans for a large building to accommodate five thousand or more.

While Pentecostalism has obviously grown during this period, it is difficult to determine whether or not church membership has kept pace with the rapid proliferation of church buildings. Church membership is not "exclusivistic" in the Caribbean and it is common for individuals to attend service at three or four different churches in any given week. Sociologists in the United States

have demonstrated that church attendance is not
always an accurate measure of church commitment
(King, 1967) and I believe that this is true also
in Trinidad where many seek to formulate a "personal" religion using several institutional
churches for inspiration; for example, Norman
Paul (Smith, 1963). Many large Pentecostal
churches on the island have fewer than fifty
members on their church roles.

The major religions in Trinidad, including
the Roman Catholic Church, have come to terms with
native beliefs concerning Obeah and/or witchcraft
(Williams, 1932; Niehoff, 1959). Such beliefs have
a long history on the islands and as Sereno suggested in 1948, may play an important role in defining Caribbean social structure. According to
Sereno, Obeah does more than provide an indirect
way of dealing with aggression, it also serves as
a universal explanation for "bad luck," and more
importantly, for success. Success is not seen as
part of the natural course of events in the
Caribbean where there is little opportunity for
upward mobility; even in a relatively advanced industrial economy such as that of Trinidad. Therefore, success must be explained in terms of supernatural or magical forces; that is, a successful
man is one who practices Obeah against his
neighbors (Beck, 1976). Success, particularly
economic success, has come to have negative
connotations in the Caribbean and this may have
ramifications for the economic development of the
area as a whole.

In Trinidad and other islands of the English-speaking Caribbean, the practice of Obeah is intimately associated with native beliefs concerning
demon possession. Obeahmen are believed to cast
demons into others in order to make them ill or to
kill them. This is usually done at someone else's
request, although occasionally an Obeahman will act
on his own behalf. It is widely believed that a
spell can be removed only by the one who placed it
or by another, more powerful, Obeahman. In either
case, "treatment" is expensive. An initial consultation with an Obeahman costs about two hundred
dollars.

Those who believe themselves to be victims of Obeah attack seek help in a number of places. Denominational ministers (Methodists, Presbyterians, Seventh Day Adventists etc.) perform exorcisms as do Catholic priests and leaders of most "syncretist" cults (Rada, Shango and the Spiritual Baptists), but Pentecostal rites are by far the most popular on the island.

There are various reasons given to account for the popularity of Pentecostal exorcism. First of all, denominational ministers and Catholic priests are said to pry into the private lives of the possessed. The Pentecostal service, to be described below, is much more anonymous and, in some cases, the possessed is able to conceal his identity successfully. Secondly, many religious leaders contend that a "good" man cannot become possessed; therefore, an element of blame is introduced as the possessed is, in some way, responsible for his own afflictions. The Spiritual Baptists, an active cult on the island, preach that a person is possessed by demons only if he is not "spiritual" enough; that is, does not devote himself to fasting and prayer (Glazier, n. d.).

The growth of Pentecostalism cannot be explained solely in terms of exorcism for much of the impetus for church growth is located outside the country. This is especially true in terms of funding. Each Pentecostal church in Trinidad is free to establish relationships with other churches on the island and overseas. Many Pentecostal churches have taken this opportunity to strengthen ties with churches in the United States and Canada at a time when other local churches have sought to become independent of outside funding and control, (e.g. the Presbyterian churches in San Fernando and surrounding towns). One church has a reciprocal relationship with Pentecostal churches in New Jersey and Pennsylvania. American churches make monthly contributions toward operating expenses of the Trinidad church and, in turn, the pastor of the Trinidad church visits the United States twice a year to perform exorcism and faith healing services.

Close ties between churches in the United States and Trinidad enable the Pentecostal church to act as an informal employment agency helping a limited number of converts obtain jobs in the United States. Some theorists, including Wedenoja (1977), suggest that these temporary labor opportunities may foster individual adjustment to the problems of modernization. Unfortunately, the types of jobs available through Pentecostal networks are not the types of jobs that promote the development of entrepreneurial skills. Is working as a domestic servant in Philadelphia or Newark really a "preadaptation" to industrial life?

Ties between Pentecostal churches in Trinidad and the United States are reflected also in values espoused from the pulpit. Trinidadian sermons emphasize sobriety, discipline, and abstinence-values which are not major concerns within the culture. The pastor's harangues against the use (or abuse) of alcohol, for example, are totally foreign to some segments of the population (Yawney, 1968; Angrosino, 1972). In addition, the church's conception of "legal" or church marriage runs counter to many beliefs and practices of the local community (Rodman, 1971; Freilich and Coser, 1972).

Sociologists, psychologists and anthropologists have found that under certain conditions the above values may "pave the way" toward upward mobility (Johnson, 1961); Rycroft (1955) considers this one of the major functions of Protestantism in the Caribbean. Angelina Pollak-Eltz, in her study of Pentecostalism in Venezuela, posits a direct relationship between the church's concern for "legal" marriage and economic advancement. She notes:

> many converts legalize their marital unions and stay with their wives. Thus family ties become stronger, as men devote more time to their wives and children. They spend more money on the improvement of their homes, and the education of their children, and

their upward mobility is greater than among other members of the lower classes (1978:481).

My research indicates that people in Trinidad do not often heed their pastor's advice. One reason may be the larger size of Trinidad churches when compared to those of Venezuela. Sermons, on the whole, are not particularly influential and I would contend that moral pronouncements from the pulpit probably have their greatest impact on the small minority within the congregation who have already adopted these particular values into their lives. Sermons serve to legitimate previously adopted behavior patterns.

The pastor frequently alludes to virtues inherent in economic success. He states clearly that "there is nothing holy about being poor!" and "when Solomon found favor with the Lord, he became a rich man." This takes away some negative connotations of wealth and, again, serves to legitimate previously adopted behavior patterns.

For many, the sermon is not a focal point of service and they are only willing to put up with it in order to gain other, more tangible, benefits from church attendance. Most church activity centers around rites of exorcism. There is a tremendous demand for such services and a large number of persons, from all over the islands and Venezuela, come each week. As mentioned above, it is possible to maintain a degree of anonymity at this service that would not be possible in a local church. This is an important consideration in determining where to go for help.

In the Curepe church, where I did the bulk of my fieldwork, exorcism services are performed twice a week. On Wednesday, exorcism service begins at nine o'clock in the morning and continues until late in the afternoon. On Friday, exorcism service begins in the early evening and lasts much of the night. Other Pentecostal churches in San Fernando and Port-of-Spain hold their services on other days of the week.

During the first two hours of the Curepe service, recorded gospel music is played while those who desire to receive the blessings of the pastor are organized into one long line. The pastor prays over the people as they pass before the altar in formation. Passing before the altar is something of a "litmus test" for the possessed. As they approach the altar they begin to quake and shout and must be restrained and returned to their seats. Of the hundreds who pass before the altar each service, only a few (five or six) are found to be victims of Obeah. The rest now know that their problems are of natural and not supernatural origin. This may be an important first step toward a natural etiology of disease.

The pastor actively encourages all who pass before the altar to seek medical attention. Until recently, a registered nurse was in attendance to make certain his advice was followed. Now, the pastor makes direct referrals to area medical practitioners. In 1978, I interviewed twenty persons who claimed to have consulted with a medical doctor under direct orders from the Curepe pastor. Of these, eleven had never gone to a doctor's office before.[5]

Services are quite long and rites of exorcism are never performed until the final hours. Before exorcism, there is much glossolalia ("speaking in tongues"), sermons, scripture readings and testimonies. Between ten and twenty testimonies are taken each week and a great deal of attention is paid to the distance that one has travelled to get to the church. (People do not use their real names during testimony). In the eyes of the congregation, a journey to the Pentecostal church is seen as a "pilgrimage" (Turner, 1973; Torrey, 1973). Such movement may play a role in the modernization process in itself by bringing about an awareness of alternatives through travel.

After the final testimony, the pastor turns to the congregation and tells them that they must praise the Lord for what they have heard here today. The congregations responds by standing, raising their hands in the air and chanting: "Praise

the Lord...Jesus..Jesus...Praise the Lord...
Jesus..Jesus...Praise the Lord...Jesus!" The
emotion builds as the pastor reminds the congregation that demons cannot bear to hear the holy
name of Jesus. In sequence, and with surprisingly little overlap, the possessed jump from
their seats screaming. Church helpers rush to
the possessed and carry them to the front of
the church. Usually, one or two new victims
(who did not go through the line earlier) are
discovered at this time.

The pastor approaches each victim individually bringing down the hand microphone from the
altar so that all may hear the possessed. The
church has an elaborate sound system which adds
considerably to the dramatic impact of exorcism.
Four questions are asked of each victim: 1) Who
sent you? 2) How many are you? 3) Why are you
in this person? and 4) How long have you been in
this person? The response, in all cases, is a
series of shrieks and garbled curses (similar to
the movie, The Exorcist, which ran in Port-of-
Spain for nearly a year).

When the demons do not respond coherently to
the pastor's questions, he seems to lose his patience. Exchanges between the pastor and the demons
are often humorous taking on an element of play:

> Pastor: I don't have any more time to waste on you, you filthy demon...now get out!
>
> Demon: Ahhggg...I want to kill her.
>
> Pastor: Why do you want to kill this sweet woman?
>
> Demon: I hate her...ahhgggg.. (curses).
>
> Pastor: Why do you hate this woman?
>
> Demon: She snores!

After five or ten minutes of banter with the demons,
the pastor grabs the victim by the throat and

commands the demon to leave "in the name of Jesus." The victim gags, sometimes spitting into a paper bag, and this is taken as a sign of the demon's departure. The pastor's major concern is making sure that all demons have left the victim. Some victims are found to be possessed by twenty demons or more.

I would contend that much of the humor and entertainment values of Pentecostal exorcism may stem from a perceived tension between traditional and modern beliefs. While Pentecostals do not deny the existence of demons, they do provide an alternate way of dealing with them. Individuals may be forced to reconsider their worldviews and, in some cases, to replace them with a more rational (Weber, 1968; Inkles and Smith, 1974) approach to the supernatural.

The Pentecostal rite fosters a modern and/or rational approach to the supernatural in several ways. It is, above all, an impersonal service. The pastor uses the same techniques on everyone and does not interfere with their daily lives. This contrasts with the approach of the Obeahman or cult healer who takes a personal interest in the life of the possessed, often trying to "run his life" telling him what to eat, when to have sex, and how to become more "spiritual."

Relations between the Pentecostal pastor and the victim are standardized and, therefore, predictable. This is a public ceremony and the pastor must conform to the congregation's and the victim's expectations. On the other hand, at a private service the victim and his family are at the complete mercy of the healer. It is the healer who defines the situation and no one knows when an unscrupulous healer will turn on a client making exorbitant demands and sending "illness" if these demands are not met.

As mentioned previously, there are also economic considerations. Pentecostal exorcism is free and the alternatives are very expensive. This, in itself, has an impact on modernization as it may alter individual attitudes toward Obeah. As means of countering Obeah attack become more accessible financially, there is less reason to fear Obeah.

Borrowing Berger's (1963) market-model, a decision to seek help in a Pentecostal church is seen as a rational choice based on a careful weighing of alternatives. The pastor and members of the congregation are aware of these alternatives and make constant reference to them in sermons and testimonies. Many members of the congregation have had personal experience with Obeahmen, Catholic priests, and denominational ministers. It can be argued in this regard that "shopping around" for an exorcist is a rational thing to do; especially when compared to the secrecy surrounding Obeah and other means of combating demonic forces.

In conclusion, it is argued that there has been considerable growth in the Pentecostal church in Trinidad but this growth is not as dramatic as the number of new buildings or rise in church attendence would lead one to believe. Much growth reflects outside sources of funding rather than indigenous support for the church.

Although the impact of the church in Trinidad is not as direct as those studied by Pollak-Eltz (1978) and Wedenoja (this volume), it does have a modernizing influence. Values espoused from the pulpit may serve to legitimate behavior that might, in some instances, lead to economic success and "pilgrimages" to Pentecostal churches may bring about an awareness of available alternatives through travel. Moreover, the church directly influences modernization by encouraging participants to seek medical attention; thus, "paving the way" toward a natural etiology of disease.

Notes

1. 'Modernization', for the purposes of this paper, is understood in terms of instrumental rationality (Weber, 1968; Inkles and Smith, 1974).

   According to Weber, action is instrumentally

rational to the extent that it: a) selects from alternative means for a given end according to a criteria of efficiency and effectiveness, and b) selects from alternative ends a specific one in terms of all possible consequences arising from its pursuit as compared with those arising from the pursuit of another one.

2. This study is based on fieldwork in Trinidad during the summers of 1976, 1977, 1978 and 1979. Fieldwork was sponsored, in part, by grants from the University of Connecticut Research Foundation and the Department of Anthropology. Much assistance was given by the National Cultural Council of Trinidad and Tobago under the direction of the late Andrew T. Carr.

   An earlier version of this paper was presented at the 1977 annual meeting of the American Anthropological Association. I wish to thank Frank Manning, Luise Margolies, Angelina Pollak-Eltz, and Felicitas D. Goodman for their helpful comments.

3. Trinidad and Tobago, Population Census Division 1961. "Population by sex, age group, and race" <u>1960 Census of the Population of Trinidad and Tobago, Preliminary Bulletin 1</u>: 2-3.

4. Trinidad and Tobago, Population Census Division, 1961. "Population by sex and religion" <u>Census Bulletin 2</u>: 2-3.

5. Often, relations between the Curepe pastor and area medical practitioners are strained. Some practitioners feel that exorcism is not an effective "treatment" for what they see as evidence for psychopathology (personal communication, Dr. Michael Beaubrun). Colleen Ward, a social psychologist, studied fifteen victims of spirit intrusion and found that only three reported stable improvement (Ward, 1979, 83). The remainder return to the Curepe church monthly or weekly for exorcism and believe that the demons will eventually return to haunt them.

References Cited

Angrosino, Michael V.
1972 Outside is Death: Alcoholism, Ideology and Community Organization Among the East Indians of Trinidad. Ph. D. Dissertation, University of North Carolina at Chapel Hill.

Beck, Jane
1976 The Implied Obeah Man. *Western Journal of Folklore* 2: 23-33.

Berger, Peter
1963 A Market Model for the Analysis of Ecumenicity. *Social Research* 30: 77-93.

Freilich, Morris and Lewis Coser
1972 Structural Imbalances of Gratification: the Case of the Caribbean Mating System. *British Journal of Sociology* 23: 11-19.

Glazier, Stephen D.
n.d. Mourning and the Articulation of Life Crisis Among the Spiritual Baptists of Trinidad. University of Connecticut: Department of Anthropology.

Herskovits, Melville J. and Frances Herskovits
1947 Trinidad Village. New York: Alfred A. Knopf.

Inkles, Alex and D. H. Smith
1974 Becoming Modern. Cambridge, Massachusetts: Harvard University Press.

Johnson, Benton
1961 Do Holiness Sects Socialize in Dominant Values? *Social Forces* 39: 309-316.

King, Morton
1967 Measuring the Religious Variable: Nine Proposed Dimensions. *Journal for the Scientific Study of Religion* 6: 173-190.

Mischel, Frances
　1957　African Powers in Trinidad: the Shango Cult. *Anthropological Quarterly* 30: 45-59.

Niehoff, Arthur
　1959　The Spirit World of Trinidad. *Shell Trinidad* 5:17-19.

Pollak-Eltz, Angelina
　1970　Shango-kult und Shouter-kirch auf Trinidad und Grenada. *Anthropos* 65: 814-832.
　1978　Pentecostalism in Venezuela. *Anthropos* 73: 461-482.

Rodman, Hyman
　1971　Lower-class Families: the Culture of Poverty in Negro Trinidad. New York: Oxford University Press.

Rycroft, W. S.
　1955　The Contribution of Protestantism in the Caribbean. *In*: A. Curtis Wilgus (edit.) The Caribbean: Its Culture; pp. 158-168. Gainesville: University of Florida Press.

Sereno, Renzo
　1948　Obeah, Magic and Social Structure in the Lesser Antilles. *Psychiatry* 11: 15-31.

Simpson, George Eaton
　1970　Religious Cults of the Caribbean: Trinidad, Jamaica and Haiti. Rio Piedras, Puerto Rico: Institute of Caribbean Studies.
　1976　Religions of the Caribbean. *In*: S. Rotberg and M. Kilson (edits), African Diaspora: Interpretive Essays. Cambridge, Massachusetts: Harvard University Press.
　1978　Black Religions in the New World. New York: Columbia.

Smith, M. G.
　1963　Dark Puritan. Kingston: University of the West Indies, Department of Extra-Mural Studies.

Torrey, E. Fuller
 1973 The Mind Game: Witchdoctors and Psychotherapists. New York: Bantam.

Turner, Victor
 1973 Pilgrim's Goal: The Center Out There. History of Religions 12: 191-230.

Ward, Colleen
 1979 Therapeutic Aspects of Exorcism. Transcultural Psychiatric Research Review 16: 82-3.

Weber, Max
 1968 Economy and Society. Roth and Wittich (edits.). London: Bedminster Press.

Wedenoja, William
 1977 Pluralism, Modernization and the Pentecostal Movement in Jamaica. Paper presented at the annual meeting of the American Anthropological Association.

Williams, J.
 1932 Voodoo and Obeahs: Phases of West Indian Witchcraft. New York: Dial Press.

Yawney, Carole
 1968 Drinking Patterns and Alcoholism Among East Indians and Negroes in Trinidad. M. A. Thesis, McGill University.

PENTECOSTALISM AND DEVELOPMENT: THE COLOMBIAN CASE

Cornelia Butler Flora
Kansas State University

Pentecostalism is a relatively new religious formation in Colombia. While the title of this paper includes the word "development", it might be more appropriate to use the phrases of proletarianization of labor and commercialization of land as suggested by Wallerstein (1976) as the precise economic shifts to be analyzed. Pentecostal growth parallels to a very large degree the shift in capitalistic development from a national bourgeoise to an international dependency capitalism. This paper relates the integration of the Colombia economy to the periphery of the world capitalist system to the emergency of Pentecostalism and relates its symbolic forms to that stage.

Data for this paper were gathered by the author in Colombia through a variety of research strategies. Two years were spent in participant observation. Systematic interviews were carried out with a sample of Pentecostals and a sample of non-Pentecostals drawn from similar neighborhoods in Palmira, Valle del Cauca. Pentecostal pastors, parish priests, non-Pentecostal Evangelical pastors and leaders of lay organizations in the Palmira inter-village system were systematically interviewed. Intensive case history interviews were carried out with over 50 leaders key in the establishment of Pentecostalism in Colombia, which were amplified through several years of correspondence. Content analysis of the major Pentecostal documents, including songs and choruses, was undertaken. Finally, analysis of church records was combined with other aggregate system level measures of the <u>municipios</u> and <u>corregimientos</u> in the region in order to undertake analysis of the structures influencing the movement's emergency and impact.

The early economic development of Colombia,

in contrast to such semi-peripheral areas such as Brazil and Chile where Pentecostalism became strong early in the 20th century, was one of isolation and nationally-based development. There was no major foreign penetration except by United States fruit interests.

In Colombia, latifundia and minifundia developed side-by-side. The large land owners were the same ones that became the urban capitalists. Thus a rural-urban split between the old and new elites did not occur. There were still substantial numbers of small farmers, although the plots were too small and population growth too large to support them on the land, forcing many Colombian peasants to leave the land. Initial rural-urban migration took place in an environment that maintained a unidimensional form of control, where the church, the polity, and the economy were tied closely together by familial ties. The old ways of viewing the universe thus remained the same, despite a change in geographic location of the masses.

Distress at conditions of oppression was manifested throughout Colombian history. But often it was diverted by the upper classes into party line warfare, rather than class line battles. The interest struggles represented by the civil War of a Thousand Days between 1889 and 1902 and the Violencia beginning in the late 1940's and lasting well into the 1960's are examples of popular uprising turned to traditional ends.

Political manifestations of popular discontent, suggested by Gaitan, emerged with General Roja Pinilla and the ANAPO Party, which represented a populist solution to Colombia's many ills. However, these beginnings of mass movements were relatively easily turned aside by the well-organized modernized elites.

Early economic development was in the hands of the rural elites, who soon became the urban-industrial elites. Natural resources, including gold, silver, tobacco, and coffee in the central part of the county remained in the hands of the traditional Colombian elites and were not exploited by foreign interests. However, in more recent times, U.S. and other foreign interests controlled the oil, which made a belated entry into the national calculus of wealth.

Foreign capital began to trickle into Colombia at the end of the War of a Thousand Days, exploiting the resources of oil, platinum, and bananas, all at the geographic margin of the Colombian state. There was early resistance to this among the workers, but the government of Colombia, at this point Liberal and committed to the idea of "development", went so far as to provide troops to put down strikes against foreign enterprises. Nevertheless, in terms of development of a national elite, foreign control and foreign investment was in the primary sector, although investment and foreign control began to flow into that sector at ever-greater rates. The secondary sector remained firmly in national hands, as did the tertiary sectors of trade and banking.

Protestant missionaries followed American capital into Colombia, but were remarkably unsuccessful, and remained, as did the capital investments, at the periphery of Colombian society. In terms of industrial development, it was Colombian capital that was the risk capital, and integration into international monopoly capitalism only occurred once the risks were taken and the enterprises were established.

The late fifties and early sixties marked the shift from domestic to foreign capital, and with it a shift from traditional utilization of both labor and land. At the same time, social dislocation was rapidly increasing with the movement from rural areas facilitating the proletarianization of labor and commercialization of the land. This rationalization of the system was reflected in the national stance toward religion. Foreign missionaries were no longer physically persecuted, and many more began entering the country, transferring almost intact North American and European images of God and modes of worship. Pentecostalism, while tracing its roots to the efforts of a few missionaries from the U.S., Canada, England, and Denmark, was more of an indigenous movement, taking on a uniquely Colombian form and manifestation. The style of the Pentecostal missionaries was quite different than that of the more middle-class missionaries of the traditional churches. These missionaries shared a working class orientation with their Colombian parishioners and were able more fully than mainstream missionaries to live among the people. Their concern was with the baptism of spirit, rather than theological sophistication. Often unprepared in the Spanish language, they instead focused on communication through the spirit and through gifts of the spirit. The symbolic initiation into Pentecostalism, speaking in tongues, often came prior to a total biblical understanding of the workings of new dynamic in theology.

Pentecostalism flourished where social dislocation was greatest and where the traditional Colombian power sectors of the church, the economy and the polity were most disorganized (Flora, 1976). It grew in areas of foreign capital penetration, which were often areas of high inmigration as well, as landless Colombian peasants sought a better way of life. Further, the individuals that became Pentecostals tended to be those that were also outside the social, economic, political, and religious nexus. They were migrants, who had migrated without the help of kin. They were outside political groups and outside mainstream economic employment. They were marginally employed and marginally tied into social networks. Pentecostalism provided for them an instant worldview explaining their situation. It also provided a supportive social network that gave each person worth and dignity in a situation that despised the poor, the dark-skinned, and the unemployed.

Immediate gratification, available in faith healing, speaking in tongues, and the belief that God is concerned with this life, right away, rather than a future life in the sweet by and by, also gave particular power to the religion. Its this worldliness, its immanence, was of crucial importance in both its initial appearance and its continuation in Colombia.

Pentecostalism's emergency in Colombia, particularly in the United Pentecostal Church (Iglesia Pentecostal Unida de Colombia) is distinct from that of the sponsoring North American Pentecostal Church. Some of the symbols remain the same, some of the hymns are translated from English to Spanish, but in translation the tune takes on a Latin beat, and different meanings are stressed. The United Pentecostal Church in the United States is a working class church, but it is even more consistent in proletarian orientation in Colombia.

In the Colombian context, different symbols are stressed. A favorite text is the one that states, "the first will be last and the last will be first." There is a feeling of confrontation. A person who is high by rank or class position is no better than the lowest, particularly those with a special power of the Holy Spirit. The feeling of the Holy Spirit giving one a special power, a special chance to work and survive in a hostile system, is in some ways reminiscent of the Ghostdance religion (Carroll, 1975), where in a situation of relative deprivation, those cut off from means of sustenance find new source of power to confront what seems to be an all powerful, irrational set of forces. In analyzing Colombian Pentecostal choruses (the songs that were sung to open and close a service and during periods of ecstasy related to prayer), I found the majority of these relate to this worldly, daily experience. They touch such themes as general joy, blessings on earth, day to day health, power given to believers, demons and the devil, and health and healing.

Most of the testimonies given by converted Pentecostals deal with the immanent nature of God sharing his power. Divine healing--a demonstration in that person of an immanent God concerned with him and his situation--is the most common theme. Testimonies analyzed stress the power of Jesus and the use of this power, through the Pentecostal faith, to solve financial difficulties and totally change lives.

The pain and suffering associated with this life are very real for Pentecostals of Colombia. There are the mighty problems of bad health, bad diet, and bad living conditions. Further, there are the emotional crises perpetuated by unstable, low incomes. A high rate of moving because of inability to pay the rent gives rise to few social ties. Family life is unstable, often a result of both bad health and low income. These are circumstances that are not unique to the transition into the world capitalist system. But the high rate of migration required by this transition makes these deprivations especially difficult.

The creation of a new type of social movement and new kinds of highly solidary groups is one response to the proletarianization of labor and the commercialization of land, especially when other avenues of response are blocked. Highly solidary groups, such as Pentecostals, with a highly focused world view, tend to construct sharp boundaries between themselves and the outside. This can be seen as hindering the multiple group interaction defining more "modern" individuals (Lerner, 1958). However, a substitution for a traditionally-based group is made. On the one hand Pentecostal membership separates them from participation in the economy and polity and may prevent them from working toward changing it. On the other hand, it predisposes them to view it with alarm, which may ultimately be used in mobilizing them toward change. Pentecostals in Colombia have very high boundary maintenance and a very strong enemy orientation.

Boundary-maintenance removes Pentecostals from community participation, which in any event is rather low among members of their social class. Many of the survey respondents felt politics was an illegitimate activity for a good Christian like a Pentecostal. However, their class position coupled with the correlation of boundary maintenance with enemy orientation tended to lead them to define the upper class as the enemy, unworthy to hold their positions of power. This predisposed them, when they did participate in politics, to vote for populist candidates, and also predisposed them on the local level to take anti-establishment actions in such things as water strikes, protection of prisoners, and other locally based protests against day-to-day living condition.

However there was little articulation of these individual sources of oppression beyond the existing sinful and unworthy ruling class. There was a recognition of the class basis of the position of the ruling elites and the oppressed.

Individuals who became Pentecostals reflect to a large degree the history of the Pentecostal movement in Colombia. They personally felt the decline in the legitimacy of the world view surrounding them and felt personal deprivation and lack of consistency in their world sphere predisposing them toward the movement. The most important variables for predicting conversion to Pentecostalism among the working class include: 1) migration due to violence, 2) migration not related to family ties, 3) occupational changes, and 4) employment by a large company. All of these indicate disassociation from a larger symbolic context and provide mechanisms for individual deviance (i.e. acceptance of the Pentecostal world view) to occur.

The link between these predispositions and becoming a Pentecostal was the method of introduction of the movement. Face to face interaction, symbolic of the later intimacy established by the movement, was critical. Invitation of a friend or relative was the first introduction for forty percent of the sample. Another large percentage were introduced to Pentecostalism through visitations to home or work place, a constant activity of Pentecostals which leads to brief face to face interactions with a large number of people in the course of their witnessing. A very small percentage came to Pentecostalism seeking solutions to particular problems. Their social situation itself was problematic, and they sought a larger understanding or world view illuminating their problems. Solution of individual problems was not the most important motivation for Colombians' initial contact with the movement, but problem solution did provide for the maintenance of movement adherence.

A typical Pentecostal is Fidelina Rojas, a woman of thirty-three years. Currently living in Palmira, she supports herself selling fruit at a stand in the <u>galeria</u> of the central market in town. She married and became a mother almost simultaneously at the age of fourteen. Her oldest son is nineteen. She bore a total of nine children although two of them died in infancy. Her youngest child is nine. Six of the seven living children live with her and one, a girl of twelve, lives with her father, from whom the mother has been separated for a number of years. The two young boys work as day laborers, and one of the youngest sons works in a shop. The fifteen year old daughter works as a maid. Originally from a small town in the department of Tolima, she has had a life of constant movement, as did her entire family. Often she was separated from her husband by financial necessity. She moved to Santander when she was twenty-four, and it was there that she became converted to Pentecostalism. After living with her seven children for several years, her husband occasionally present, a passing neighbor invited her to attend a Pentecostal service. She attended, was convinced of the message, and converted. Her husband did not share her enthusiasm for the new faith and made that separation a permanent one. After that she moved several more times, looking for a cheaper place and a way to support herself and her brood. Her original job was in domestic service work, as a maid. Finally when she moved to Palmira she was able to obtain capital, buy a small place in the galeria, and sell fruit. She feels that with all her children working, she is able to make a decent income.

She is quite apolitical, feeling the church should be separated from worldly things. She believes strongly in the power of God to help her financially, as well as to solve all of the problems of the world. She did not vote prior to 1968, because she separated herself from worldly things. By the 1970 election, local church members received a revelation that they should vote, and she, like the other Pentecostals, voted for Rojas Pinilla, the Populist candidate of the ANAPO party. By becoming a Pentecostal, she found a peace and happiness that she never had before. Despite her separation from her husband and the fact that she has to live with her mother in very crowded circumstances, she feels that she has a good life.

There is much opposition to her Pentecostalism. Her family has not been favorable to her church attendance. In her small room that houses the entire family, she is not allowed to manifest her religion by hanging the usual Pentecostal Bible verses and pictures on the walls. Still, she feels that it is a good place to live because it is near the church.

She attends every service and evangelizes for the church whenever she has a chance. This occurs very often in her job, where she meets a lot of people. She says that now she is able to confide in God, and ask him questions when necessary. Before this, she did not have anyone to turn to.

Fidelina feels she is like the rest of the poor people who make up the Pentecostal Church in Colombia. The greatest problem for Colombia, in her mind, is the economy. But she finds it difficult to explain why the economy has evolved the way it has. She strongly agrees that the country is run by a group of rich people who do not have any interest in poor people, but also feels that large companies are fair to their employees. She believes that good Christians will do well in their work and anticipates that she will be treated fairly. In addition, she believes that good Christians should not belong to political parties or unions and should separate themselves from any other group that might possibly interfere with their spiritual lives. She feels that when a church becomes preoccupied with political problems of a country, it forgets the Christian life. As a result, the church becomes embroiled in the world and threatened with destruction. She does not accept the traditional Catholic dogma that her social status is God given, yet she does not feel it is useful, or even legitimate, to try to change her situation.

In looking at the emergence of Pentecostalism as related to the transition from national bourgeoise capital development to fuller integration into the world capitalist system, my basic stance is one of stressing macro-structural variables as opposed to psychological variables as explanations for social change. Nevertheless I did try to look at some of the psychological variables others associate with development to see if Pentecostalism produced them among its adherents. There seems to be no increase in acquisition of wealth or material possessions between Pentecostals and non-Pentecostals, nor was there a difference in increase of income. When asked to describe their material and income situations five years previously, neither group showed any marked improvement relative to each other. Interestingly, the material acquisition pattern of Pentecostals was quite different from that of Catholics, reflecting the primacy of their religious world view rather than complete integration into the margins of consumer society. Further, it was found that Pentecostals and non-Pentecostals alike tended not to equate economic success with spiritual downfall. As far as the Protestant ethic giving rise to independence training or entrepreneurship, it is true that most Pentecostals tend to be in business for themselves. However, many of these same people felt that being employed in a large company was a far better economic choice for life. It can readily be argued that at this stage of multi-national capitalist development, the single entrepreneur is an anachronism, rather than the bulwark of progress.

Achievement motivation was not measured directly in the study using McClelland's techniques (McClelland, 1961). However, I did ask each respondent if they intended to change their job or were looking forward to having a different or a better job in the future. Catholics, Protestants, and Pentecostalists were equally likely to see a change in job, mainly because of the bad conditions of their current one. However, Pentecostals were much more likely to see their new jobs related to the church particularly in becoming a pastor or worker. Pentecostalism provided an alternate status structure rather than a means of upward mobility within the established one. It did not provide the motivation to change the existing status hierarchy. Catholics were more likely to want to obtain upward mobility. Their aspirations were primarily in terms of owning their own business. Neither group could be viewed as revolutionary, but each could be viewed as adaptive to the margins of a nation in transition to the increasing proletarianization of labor and commercialization of land. Both are resistant to this trend rather than facilitating it. Neither group provides the personnel for the expanding middle class needed to fit traditional development theory. But that is a problem of the containing social structure, not of the individual motivations of religious adherents.

On other individual levels of modernization, Pentecostal adherence offers no clear cut contribution, either. Pentecostals are less exposed to mass media because of the constraints of boundary maintenance, although they were as aware of international and national affairs as their neighbors. They had few extended family ties, but were less socially isolated than Catholics of the same socio-economic status. They measured considerably higher in religiosity and salience of religion in everyday life--not surprising, given their generally highly focused world view. When they were in nuclear families, their role structure tended to be more egalitarian, due not to a conscious desire to liberate women, but to an emphasis on the priesthood of all believers, which provided alternative mechanisms for status attainment for women within the family. Like Lerner (1958), I found no single dimension of modernity--nor were any of the sub-dimensions predictive of other change-related dimensions. Individual-level sources of change, of development, seem not only irrelevant to development in a structure such as that of Colombia, a country in transition to the proletization of labor and the commercialization of land, they also appear to have little internal validity.

REFERENCES CITED

Carroll, Michael P.
  1975 Revitalization Movements and Social Structure: Some Quantitative Tests. *American Sociological Review*. 40 389-401.

Flora, Cornelia Butler
  1976 *Pentecostalism in Colombia: Baptism by Fire and Spirit*. Rutherford, N.J.: Fairleigh Dickinson University Press.

Lerner, Daniel
  1958 *The Passing of Traditional Society*. New York: The Free Press.

McClelland, David
  1961 *The Achieving Society*. New York: The Free Press.

Wallerstein, Immanuel
  1976 From Feudalism to Capitalism: Transition or Transitions? *Social Forces*. 55 273-283.

THE POWER OF PENTECOSTALISM IN A BELIZEAN VILLAGE

Donna Birdwell-Pheasant

Descriptions of the conditions preceding major religious changes or religious movements invariably refer to the people's loss of a sense of control over the important elements of their existence, a feeling that their lives have become unpredictable, meaningless, unsatisfying.[1] Such a sense of powerlessness may be an inherent part of the process of modernization (Adams 1974: 53; 1975: 312). As the power exercised by a central government increases, the power reserved to individuals and local communities appears more and more insignificant by comparison. Ordinary individuals become increasingly impotent to effect (or even affect) the decisions that structure their daily lives (Adams 1974: 45-46; 1975: 299).

This loss of relative power contributes to a loss of self-esteem and a dissatisfaction with the old social identities and social memberships. Reclaiming power requires new forms of individual and group organization and integration. Individuals or small groups (such as families) may band together to pool their declining power. They may also find ways to gain access to the newly-formed reservoirs or centers of power at the upper levels of the power structure.

This paper will focus on religion as a force for motivating new identities (or strengthening old ones) that redefine (or reaffirm) the boundaries of social groups, thereby enhancing the individual's or group's exercise of and access to power. The problem will be examined in terms of the history of religious and social change in the little village of Chunox in northern Belize,[2] where Pentecostalism is only one of several religious forces at work.

Background of Chunox

Chunox was settled in the last half of the 19th century by refugees from the Caste Wars in Yucatan (Birdwell 1979; Reed 1964). The settlers were predominantly from the "mestizo" ethnic stratum of Yucatecan society, the middle sector that stood in contrast to the "whites" (Spanish) above and the "real indians" (the rebels and other "backwoods" Maya) below (Barabas 1976: 21). These mestizo-class people found all that they needed in Chunox--good land for farming, good water, and wage work readily available on two nearby sugar <u>ranchos</u> that had been opened by families of "white" Yucatecan refugees.

Chunox society was then, as now, organized primarily in terms of the patrilaterally extended family. But at this time it was also a stratified society, with the sugar <u>rancheros</u> at the top, some mid-level supervisory personnel, and a lower-stratum majority combining labor on the ranchos with subsistence-level agricultural production on rented or common land.

The religious background was a blend of folk Catholic and native Mayan beliefs and practices, with the upper social stratum being more Catholic than Maya in its religion. The greatest emphasis in rituals was on <u>novenas</u>--nine-day prayer cycles for one of the ten or so locally owned saints--rather than on Maya ceremonies of field and forest (Redfield and Villa Rojas 1962). The structure of religious life was based on the <u>novenarios</u>, the nine-member groups responsible for making novenas and fiestas for the respective saints. Leadership of the novenario fell to a senior member of the family who owned the saint, with the rest of the group normally recruited along kinship lines. The most important saints were those owned by the sugar rancheros and bosses. Participation in novenas and fiestas extended to the whole village and beyond.

The novena and fiesta complex had little to do with institutional Catholicism. The primary link with the Catholic Church was the priest, who made infrequent and irregular visits to Chunox.

The priest was revered for his privy knowledge of the word of God (important portions of which were delegated to the people through catechism) and his exclusive authority to perform baptisms, confirmations, and marriages.

Sometime in the early 1900s, the sugar ranchos folded (mainly due to competition from a mechanized factory) and Chunoxeños turned to chicle-bleeding and mahogany-cutting as sources of wages, further deemphasizing agriculture. The chicle and mahogany bosses proved to be severe taskmasters, imposing strict regulations on the use of forested land for agriculture. Forestry work sometimes required the men to travel great distances and to be away from home for long periods of time. Family life suffered, as indicated by the numerous broken marriages and adulterous liaisons reported for this period. In 1916 a hurricane hit northern Belize, followed in 1918 by an epidemic of Spanish influenza which, according to the records of the Catholic priests, claimed as much as 30 percent of the population in some villages.

In the wake of these social disruptions and natural economic disasters, missionaries of the Seventh Day Adventist Church arrived in Chunox. They gave Bibles to the people (few of whom could read) in an effort to sever their dependence on the priest for access to the word of God. The missionaries told Chunoxeños that they must give up praying to Maya deities and spirits and to the "sticks of wood and pieces of pottery" they called saints--to cease, as the missionaries saw it, serving the devil. The missionaries did not follow up on their initial success by organizing a congregation of believers in Chunox and the commitment to Adventism was short-lived. The tithe and abstention from eating pork and from working on Saturday proved to be unrealistic demands, in serious conflict with local custom and necessity.

The only lasting effect of the encounter with Adventism was a severe culture loss. Although most people again took up the forms of the old religion, they were now empty forms, shorn of their vitality and meaning. Some few families apparently resisted the Adventist inroads; they remain traditional Catholics to the present day. Nevertheless, the power of Catholicism to integrate the village into a cohesive unit had been lost.

The collapse of the sugar ranchos contributed to the leveling of social strata in Chunox. The process was futher advanced during the 1920s when the lower-stratum Maya-speaking villagers gave up their indian language in favor of the Spanish language associated with their former patrons and bosses.

Dependence on chicle and mahogany work came to an abrupt end in 1956 with another more severe hurricane, which devastated the village and the surrounding forest. The owners of the denuded land put it up for sale, and the government bought a little over four square kilometers for Chunox. Much of the rest was purchased by an entrepreneur from the southwestern United States who arrived in 1958 to set up a cotton ranch where one of the sugar ranchos had been. Wage work was once again available. But the cotton enterprise was ill-fated, for in 1963 the cowboy-patron was arrested in the United States for allegedly smuggling illegal drugs. Chunoxeños found themselves shamed by association and left to their own devices more completely than ever before. It was about this time that Seventh Day Adventism experienced a fleeting revival in Chunox.

Although Chunoxeños still owned no land, they turned to agriculture with new intensity, freely exploiting the land of the now absentee landlord. But they soon found the vagaries of a government-controlled market system, mediated by exploitative produce brokers, as unpredictable and burdensome as any sugar ranchero or chicle boss had ever been.

The only wage work available in recent years[3] has been in the cane fields of the western half of Belize's northern district, where a sugar boom in the 1960s produced significant advances in the standard of living of many independent small farmers. Chunoxeños were excluded from this boom because they lacked any means of getting cane to the factory--there is no road into Chunox and the water route is navigable only by the smallest shallow-draft vessels. Other forms of government patronage--land grants, home loans, agricultural improvement loans, health services, etc.--have also reached the cane-farming villages, heightening Chunox's sense of isolation and abandonment.

Recent Religious Change

When I first arrived in Chunox in the summer of 1974, there were three main religious groups in the village. A small group of traditional Catholics still managed to carry on the syncretic Maya-Catholic folk religion, albeit in a much diluted form. For most Chunoxeños, however, the viability of that faith had been lost in the encounter with Adventism in the 1920s when, as they put it, "our eyes were opened." Most of those so disillusioned, with their descendants, formed a group that we may call the "nominal Catholics." Members of this group still call themselves Catholics, but feel more enlightened than their more traditional brethren, since they pray neither to saints nor to Maya spirits--in fact, they rarely pray at all.

The third group had evolved out of the second Adventist mission effort of the 1960s. When this new generation of converts once again felt the lifestyle incompatibilities of Adventism, they did not return to Catholicism, even nominally. Instead, they turned to another brand of Protestantism, the Church of the Nazarene. In 1974, the Nazarene congregation claimed 16 members, who exhibited varying degrees of enthusiasm and commitment.

In autumn 1974, yet another hurricane hit northern Belize, destroying much of the corn and fruit crops for the season. It was accompanied by flooding, followed by an unusually long dry season. Although the dry season normally ends in May, this one stretched into September of 1975. During this period of hardship, one young Nazarene man returned to Adventism and, in the months that followed, converted most of his patrilateral family.

At the height of the drought, the remaining Nazarenes sponsored a revival meeting or "campaña" in Chunox, which attracted almost 200 enthusiastic participants from as far away as the Guatemalan Petén. This was Chunox's first direct contact with such groups as evangelical free churches, Christadelphians, and Pentecostals, although their messages had been heard via radio. The Nazarenes, during this event, began calling themselves "evangélicos," a term that they saw as including all of the participating religious faiths. By the end of August, the evangélicos of Chunox claimed a membership of 24, despite the loss of four of the original 16 Nazarenes.

The revitalized religious fervor of these evangélicos brought with it a desire for a chapel of their own, which they had begun to build in August 1975, according to the style of traditional Maya housing. But the Nazarene church proved uncooperative in this effort, while the Pentecostal Church of God offered not only to provide all the necessary building materials, but to provide Chunox with its own pastor as well. Thus, by mid-1976 there were no longer any Nazarenes in Chunox, no evangélicos, but rather a strong and enthusiastic congregation of Pentecostals, putting the final touches to their modern concrete-floored, lumber-walled chapel. The Pentecostals numbered 26, having lost four members and added six, including the new pastor and his wife.

In early 1976, the Catholic Church had sent two Chunoxeños to a lay-leaders training session in Honduras. Upon their return, they organized a small group known locally as the "hermanos católicos," the Catholic brothers. This nascent movement has drawn members from the ranks of both traditional and nominal Catholics.

Analysis

Chunox's 164 adult inhabitants[4] owe their loyalties to five different religious groups--the traditional Catholics, Seventh Day Adventists, nominal Catholics, Catholic brothers, and Pentecostal Church of God. We have seen how these various groups came to exist in Chunox; we now turn to an analysis of the groups themselves--their membership and how they serve the social needs of their members.

TRADITIONAL CATHOLICS. The traditional Catholic group draws almost 85 percent of its 27 members from four inter-related families. It has no formal leader, relying instead on the structure of the families involved. The primary traditional Catholic families also represent the core of a political faction that stands in opposition to another family-based faction that controls the local Village Council. Thus, an identification as traditional Catholic heightens the sense of separateness from the Village Council group (all of whom are nominal Catholic, Catholic brothers, or Protestants) and fosters internal cohesiveness. This out-faction also articulates with traditionalists in other villages. Its primary political patron is a Senator from the northern district who has preached socialism and political activism to the dispossessed (Jones 1971: 25ff) and whose home village produced a "conscious effort...to stage a modest revival...of Maya culture" (Jones 1971: 62).

SEVENTH DAY ADVENTISTS. The Adventist congregation draws six of its eight formal members from one extended family. The head of this family is a former Village Council chairman who has strong ambitions to advance his family's socio-economic status. The main religious strength of the Adventists lies in the son who was a Nazarene in 1974. It was his strong family ties that prohibited his becoming a key member of the Nazarene or Pentecostal group, for reasons we shall discuss shortly. The final two members of the Adventists are the present Village Council chairman and his wife.

All of the Adventists are of above-average economic means, a factor which permits them to observe such requirements as the tithe, food restrictions and abstinence from work on Saturdays. They are a relatively self-sufficient group, relying little on outside religious support or contacts. As might be expected, their primary extra-village ties are political.

NOMINAL CATHOLICS. The 90 nominal Catholics are essentially a residual group of those who have not chosen to exploit any religious power base. Not surprisingly, the nominal Catholics are dominant within the official Village Council faction and most have had more than ordinary economic success.

CATHOLIC BROTHERS. The Catholic brothers draw seven of their eleven members from the Chunox schoolteachers and their families. All four of the teachers in Chunox's Catholic-affiliated school are native Chunoxeños who, despite their youth, form an "educated elite" within the village. As such, they find folk Catholicism personally unsuitable. The remaining four members of the Catholic brothers are from a family which maintains a residence in Belize City as well as in Chunox; this urban orientation makes them perpetual semi-strangers in Chunox.

The Catholic brothers have entrusted leadership to the two men who attended the lay leaders' conference and to the head schoolteacher. These men also receive delegated power from the Catholic Church. The group articulates its members with the Catholic Church as institution and, thus, with the urban centers of Belize, where the political and commercial elites are predominantly of the Catholic faith and alumni of Catholic schools.

PENTECOSTALS. The Pentecostal congregation draws its 28 members from three sources: 16 come from broken or weak patrilateral families; eight are occupants of low-status positions within more powerful families; and four are outsiders with no kin in Chunox at all. The Pentecostal congregation, then, is not a basis for solidifying an inter-family political alliance, as is traditional Catholicism; it is not a springboard for the upwardly mobile, as is the Catholic brotherhood; neither is it being used, as is Adventism, as an adjunct power base for the local ascendancy of one family. It is, rather, a substitute for the family itself, an alliance of individuals marginalized by the structuring of local village life in terms of the family.

The ties of brotherhood and sisterhood within the Pentecostal group are quite strong, competing effectively with, and sometimes overshadowing, blood sibling ties. These facts not only explain part of the attractiveness of Pentecostalism for its members, but also help us understand why some individuals have left the congregation and why others, although sympathizing with Pentecostal beliefs, have not joined and probably will not join. Key members of strong families not only do not need the additional social ties, but also can be effectively dissuaded from entering into the demanding personal obligations of Pentecostal brotherhood by application of familial sanctions.

Local church organization centers on the pastor and a hierarchy of deacons and lesser church officials, all of whom serve at the pleasure of the entire voting congregation. The primary qualifications for office are service and charisma, traits that are theoretically achievable by all.

The Pentecostal church as national and international institution is characterized by its acephalous, reticulate organization (Gerlach and Hine 1968: 26). The various congregations are linked by the same ties of fictive kinship that link the members of a local congregation with one another. In Belize, the common identity of all members of the Pentecostal Church of God is facilitated by certain shared characteristics beyond the common faith. The Pentecostal Church of God is predominantly an Indian-mestizo organization in which Anglo missionaries maintain a consistently low profile. In a country where most of the Protestant sects--including the Nazarenes, Adventists, and another variety of Pentecostals-- are dominated by Anglo missionaries and urban black Creoles, only the Pentecostal Church of God offers an alternative to Catholicism that facilitates maintenance of Indian-mestizo ethnic boundaries.

Conclusions

Religious affiliations allow Chunoxeños to pool their individual or family power and to gain access to external sources of power. Only the nominal Catholics do not use religious affiliation in this way; but their strong political ties serve a similar purpose. The Adventists, too, use politics to tap outside power centers; their religion is a means of pooling power to be exercised locally.

For all the other groups, however, articulation with the outside world through religion seems to be of paramount importance. And all manage to effect it without violating ethnic boundaries.

The Catholic brothers have integrated themselves into the bottom level of the vertical structure of institutional Catholicism. The traditional Catholics, on the other hand, use religion as a basis of political opposition to the established order and their articulation to the outside is more horizontal. It is true that they have a political patron, but he is a politician whose main power has derived from his charismatic appeal as a man of the people. Traditional Catholicism, with its emphasis on rituals that have always been fairly independent of the Church and with its nativistic tendencies, operates in the interstices of the official institutional order.

Pentecostalism is also a horizontally-articulating, interstitial movement. But it is a passive movement, fostering resignation rather than instigating change. Nevertheless, it has a definite structural impact. The power of religion to affect social structure and to mediate dilemmas of identity and powerlessness lies in its ability to motivate strong personal identification with the religious group. And in this, the power of Pentecostalism would seem to be unsurpassed.

Through its fictive kin ties, egalitarian ideals, and charismatic leadership, Pentecostalism links people of low status into unified blocks. But each such unit in the "reticulate, ace phalous" Pentecostal church may respond, within certain limits, to its own situation in its own way. Pentecostals are prejudiced neither wholly in favor of modernization (as the nominal Catholics, Adventists, and Catholic brothers tend to be) nor wholly against it (as the traditional Catholics tend to be). Thus, in its capacity for cultural innovation, the Pentecostals represent a potentially powerful operating unit in the structure of Chunoxeño and Belizean society.

FOOTNOTES

1. Barber, in 1941, noted that messianic movements generally spring from "the widespread experience of 'deprivation'--the despair caused by inability to obtain what the culture has defined as the ordinary satisfactions of life" (1972: 513). Linton's classic 1943 essay on "Nativistic Movements" focused especially on conditions of subordination and inferiority (1972: 501). Another classic, Wallace's 1956 article on "Revitalization Movements," cited the "diminution of... efficiency in satisfying needs" and resultant cultural distortion as the conditions leading to revitalization (1972: 506-507). In 1962, Aberle summarized such socio-cultural milieux in terms of "relative deprivation," which he defined as "a negative discrepancy between legitimate expectation and actuality" (1972: 528). And LaBarre, in his 1971 survey of the field, although he demurred in positing any single cause for religious movements, apparently had no difficulty in classing a very broad variety of them under the rubric of "crisis" (1971).

2. Research was carried out in the summers of 1974 and 1975 with funding by the Cerro Maya Foundation, Dallas, Texas, and in July 1976 through January 1977 through a grant received from the Department of Anthropology, Southern Methodist University, Dallas.

3. Since 1975, additional seasonal employment has been available at an archeological site near Chunox.

4. An "adult," by local standards, is an individual 15 years of age or older. The total population of Chunox in December 1976 was 375.

REFERENCES

Aberle, David
    1972   "A Note on Relative Deprivation Theory as Applied to Millenarian and Other Cult Movements," 527-531 in William A. Lessa and Evon Z. Vogt, eds., Reader in Comparative Religion: An Anthropological Approach (Third Edition), New York: Harper and Row.

Adams, Richard N.
    1974   "Harnessing Technological Development," 37-68 in John J. Poggie and Robert N. Lynch, eds., Rethinking Modernization: Anthropological Perspectives, Westport, Conn.: Greenwood Press.

    1975   Energy and Structure: A Theory of Social Power, Austin: University of Texas Press.

Barabas, Alicia
    1976   "Identidad Étnica y Estratificación en Yucatán," manuscript, Centro Regional del Sureste, INAH, Mexico.

Barber, Bernard
    1972   "Acculturation and Messianic Movements," 512-515 in Lessa and Vogt (op cit).

Birdwell, Donna
    1979   Cycles of Power: Social Organization in a Belizean Village, Ph. D., Southern Methodist University; University Microfilms.

Gerlach, Luther P. and Virginia H. Hine
    1968   "Five Factors Crucial to the Growth and Spread of a Modern Religious Movement," *Journal for the Scientific Study of Religion* 7: 23-40.

Jones, Grant D.
    1971   "The Politics of Agricultural Development in Northern British Honduras," Developing Nations Monograph Series One, No. IV, Winston-Salem, N.C.: Overseas Research Center, Wake Forest University.

LaBarre, Weston
    1971   "Materials for a History of Studies of Crisis Cults: A Bibliographic Essay," *Current Anthropology* 12: 3-44.

Linton, Ralph
    1972   "Nativistic Movements," 497-503 in Lessa and Vogt (*op cit*).

Redfield, Robert and Alfonso Villa Rojas
    1962   *Chan Kom: A Maya Village*, Chicago: University of Chicago Press.

Reed, Nelson
    1964   *The Caste War of Yucatán*, Stanford: University Press.

Wallace, Anthony F. C.
    1972   "Revitalization Movements," 503-512 in Lessa and Vogt (*op cit*).

PENTECOSTALISM: A REVOLUTIONARY OR CONSERVATIVE MOVEMENT?

Judith Chambliss Hoffnagel
Universidade Federal de Pernambuco

The growth of Pentecostalism has constituted one of the important features of Brazilian religious life during the last two decades. In 1974 Brazil's 2,950,000 Pentecostals accounted for well over half of the total number of Protestants in the country and it is estimated that at its current rate of growth (80% per decade) the Pentecostal community will number 34 million by the year 2004 (Read, 1967:179).[1] The phenomenal growth of Pentecostalism has taken place during a period marked by an increased pace of industrialization, a rationalization of export agriculture and a demographic shift from rural to urban areas. There is undoubtedly a relationship between these changes and the increased membership of Pentecostal churches. The dynamics of this relationship, however, remain somewhat unclear. Some scholars have viewed Pentecostalism as part of a more generalized rebellion by the expanding urban lower classes against the traditional forms of social relationships associated with an agrarian, patriarchal society. Melvin (1970:189), for example, claims that those rural migrants who join a Pentecostal group are "engaging in effective protest of upper class paternalism." Willems (1964:103) has stated that "conversion to Protestantism, especially its sectarian varieties constitutes one of the many ways in which hostility and rebellion against a decaying social structure may be expressed" and labels the Pentecostal movement "a form of symbolic rebellion against the social status quo."

Utilizing data gathered during a two-year study of the Assembléia de Deus in the Northeastern state of Pernambuco, this paper will attempt to demonstrate that Pentecostalism should be viewed, not as a rebellion against the traditional social order or upper class paternalism, but rather as a conservative social force, tending to strengthen rather than weaken traditional forms of social organization. An examination of both the internal structure of the Assembléia de Deus--Brazil's largest Pentecostal church--and the way in which it articulates with the dominant power structure reveals that the Pentecostal community bears a striking resemblance to the traditional plantation society.

In Brazil, as in the rest of Latin America, the large landed estate played an instrumental role in forging the social relationships and cultural values that have characterized the traditional social order. According to Medina (1964:30), the large landed estate created a social structure in which customs crystalized around:

> Belief in the warm value of human relationships, belief in the support which should not be lacking in any moment of crisis and belief in the unknown and therefore unlimited power of the chief.

In the Brazilian Northeast this social structure emerged during the colonial period when large patriarchal families controlled the coastal sugar plantations and the cattle ranches in the interior. Individuals would attach themselves to one of these powerful families and submit to the guidance and authority of the patron in return for physical protection and economic security otherwise unobtainable.

The authority exercised by the head of the patriarchal family, or patrão, rests on the belief that he would not fail to protect members of the social unit should a crisis occur. In return for such protection absolute loyalty to the patrão is required. Those who betrayed such loyalty paid a high price. Social ostracism, economic sanctions, petty harassment from authorities, and even violence and death were employed by the patrão to punish dissident members of his clientele. Hutchinson (1966:4) believes that this social pattern is so deeply ingrained in the Brazilian culture that it has created a population of dependents, a population that lacks iniative and one that is extremely submissive to authority.

The assertion that conversion to Pentecostalism constitutes an expression of "hostility and rebellion" against the traditional social order rests on several assumptions. First, it has been claimed that Pentecostalism has experienced its greatest growth in those areas most effected by urbanization and industrialization. Thus in 1960, the Southeast of Brazil (the states of Minas Gerais, Paraná, Espírito Santo, Guanabara, Rio de Janeiro, and São Paulo), the so-called industrial states, contained 44% of the total population and 49.4% of the total number of Protestants, while the Northeast, an area which experienced little industrial growth contained 31% of the national population and only 11.6% of the total number of Protestants. It has also been suggested that the internal structure of Protestant churches, especially the Pentecostal sects, characterized by lay leadership, active participation of all members and spiritual equality regardless of social class, represents a sharp contrast to the rigidly structured and authoritarian Catholic church that permeated Brazil's traditional rural society. According to Willems (1964:103), the very success of Pentecostalism compared to the Historic Protestant churches[2] stems from the fact that the former is ideologically and organizationally furtherest removed from the structure of the traditional society.

A closer examination of the statistical evidence, however, indicates that in terms of the growth of Protestantism, and by extension, Pentecostalism, there is no significant difference between the "backward" Northeast and the industrial heartland of the South. Whereas in 1970 Protestants accounted for 5.7% of the population of São Paulo, Brazil's most industrialized state, they made up 4.6% of the inhabitants of Pernambuco, a state characterized by plantation agriculture and the absence of industry. Moreover, if we were to discount the relatively large number of Protestants descended from European immigrants found in São Paulo,[3] the small difference of 1.1% between São Paulo and Pernambuco would diminish even further. Moreover, data for Pernambuco reveal that the rural portion of the state contains a larger percentage (59%) of Protestants than the state capital (41%).[4]

The internal structure of Recife's Assembléia de Deus, rather than offering a sharp contrast to that of the traditional society, tends to reproduce it. For one thing, like other religious groups that call upon the individual to sever most ties with the outside world, Pentecostalism creates a relatively closed community not unlike that of the subordinate population on a traditional plantation.[5] True enough, an individual makes an independent decision to join the Assembléia, but once he does so he must submit to the will of the group and those in authority. One way in which the church asserts its control over the individual is to limit his contacts with the larger society. Hence the Assembléia prohibits those not already married at the time of baptism from marrying non-Pentecostals. Those who fail to adhere to this rule face immediate expulsion. The Assembléia also prohibits its members from engaging in activities common to the vast majority of Brazilians--social drinking, gambling, attending movies and sporting events, frequenting public beaches, and participation in Carnaval. Since members of the church, especially those of long standing, have a limited social life outside the church, expulsion cuts them off from the only community they know.

The Assembléia de Deus has developed an elaborate and effective mechanism for impeding breaches of discipline. Gossip concerning instances of deviant behavior is fairly common and reports of transgressions usually find their way to the disciplinary commissions in each local congregation. These commissions call on alleged infractors to justify their actions, and if warranted will issue a formal warning. Should the warning not be heeded, or if the infraction is of a serious nature, individual cases are taken before a special disciplinary board headed by the <u>pastor presidente</u> which meets monthly in the <u>matriz</u> or central church. The investigations of the disciplinary commissions invariably become public knowledge and wayward individuals receive immediate feedback of disapproval from their peers. Those who heed neither the warnings of the board or the advice and urgings of friends, find themselves expelled from the church.

  Those who see the internal structure of the Pentecostal churches as the antithesis of rigidly structured social organizations characterized by sharp lines of authority between a dominant elite and subordinate groups, point out that leadership positions in Pentecostal churches are achieved rather than ascribed and that leaders come from the membership itself. Thus, the lack of distance between church leaders and their following allows the latter to place limits on the actions of the former. My examination of the Assembléia de Deus, however, makes it clear that 1) the majority of church members have little to say in the selection of leaders, 2) members perceive of church leaders as "superior", and 3) church leaders exercise an inordinate amount of authority and influence over the lives of their followers.

  While all leadership positions are theoretically open to the entire male membership of the Assembléia, top positions are filled only after years of apprenticeship in minor posts. It is the leadership itself which decides upon new appointments and promotions. More importantly, the <u>pastor presidente</u>, constitutes one of the salient features of the Assembléia's internal organization. This fact was brought home to me countless times during the course of my research. Permission to attend church cults depended entirely on the will of the pastor. Church leaders refused to answer questions about themselves or the Assembléia without first contacting the pastor presidente, and members were reluctant to submit to interviews before receiving assurances that my work enjoyed the approval of the pastor.

The church community conforms closely to the traditional model of an extended family in which the patrão dispenses aid and support and in return receives obedience and loyalty, which at times can border on devotion, from his followers. Church leaders, especially the pastor presidente, serve as a source of aid in the resolution of individual problems. A husband may, for example, complain that his wife, perhaps because she wants no more children, refuses to comply with her wifely duties. Wives, on the other hand, will seek the support of the pastor in order to curb their husband's extra-marital activities. There can be no question that the pastor can exercise a decisive influence on the lives of his followers. One case involving a young man torn between defying his parents by studying for the university entrance exams rather than getting a job, became the subject of public testimony at a weekly prayer meeting. The young man in question, after describing the period of anguish and anxiety through which he had passed, testified that "my pastor gave me the courage to try and enter the university." This incident not only illustrates the pastor's role as counselor, but demonstrates how examples of his wise counsel reverberate through the church community, thereby increasing his moral authority. In come cases, the church official's role as counselor requires him to act as a broker between the individual and the larger society. It is not uncommon for pastors and other officials to help members find employment. Moreover, in their role of administrator, church officials have acquired considerable experience in dealing with local, state, and federal bureaucracies. Thus, it is not surprising that they are sometimes called upon to aid members in dealing with the government. This usually involves assisting members in securing government retirement benefits and access to national health care.

It is, however, the pastor's spiritual powers, that is, his ability to preach, heal, speak in tongues, and receive the Holy Spirit, that primarily accounts for the hold he exercises over church members.[6] Although the Assembléia's ideology proclaims that all are spiritually equal in the eyes of God, the pastor is clearly regarded as superior in the eyes of his followers. Members of the Assembleia hold the pastor presidente in great reverence. His framed photograph constitutes a prized possession in many members' homes. Celebrations taking place at any of the Assembléia's temples are not considered a true success unless the pastor puts in a personal appearance. To have conversed with the pastor becomes a source of prestige to individual members who will proudly repeat his words to family and friends. Both the anniversary of his assuming the position of pastor presidente and his birthday are celebrated as major occasions during which numerous church members present him with gifts. Although there are more than 25,000 active members in Recife's Assembleia, individuals conceive of a personal relationship between themselves and the pastor presidente. During the course of my field work I rarely heard the expression "the pastor" or "our pastor." Instead, members would invariably refer to the leader of the Assembléia as "meu pastor."

Like traditional wielders of power and authority in Brazil, the pastor presidente zealously guards against the emergence of potential rivals. Indeed, the Assembléia de Deus is organized in such a way as to sharply reduce the possibility of rival leaders assuming control of any of the church's individual congregations. Thus the local congregations have no permanent leaders. Church officials-- pastors, evangelists, presbyterians, deacons--are rotated from congregation to congregation on a weekly basis, thereby reducing the chances of any one leader gathering a personal following. Moreover, all financial contributions are turned over to the matriz which controls their dispersal. These contributions, it should be noted, are quite substantial. In 1974 the Sunday School collections alone, amounted to approximately one hundred thousand dollars.

This does not mean, however, that the Assembléia has remained immune from the problem of internal schisms. Congregations have, indeed, broken away from the Assembléia de Deus in order to form independent churches. It must be pointed out, however, that splits do not reflect an anti-authoritarian spirit on the part of the church members. Most schisms that have occurred in the Assembléia de Deus have come about as the result of a younger church leader who, faced with diminishing chances of promotion as he moves up the church hierarchy, challenges the incumbent pastor whose position he seeks. Moreover, most breakaway sects, such as Manoel Melo's, Brasil para Cristo, are even more personalistic and authoritarian than the Assembleia itself.

Not only does the pastor exercise the role of the traditional patrão within the church itself, but he conditions the way in which the church articulates with the dominant political power structure. Although most church leaders emphasized that the church had little interest in politics, the Assembléia does play a role in national political life. For one thing, members of the Assembléia, like all Brazilian citizens, are required by law to vote. Moreover, like other organizations in Brazil, the Assembléia finds it useful to maintain direct links to the political elites, and members of the church have served in both Recife's city council and in the state legislature. These officials have facilitated the granting of building and parade permits, secured public lighting and paved streets for areas adjacent to the church's temples, and have found municipal and state jobs for a number of church members. Finally, the church is highly conservative. One church official who had insisted that the Assembléia had little interest in politics, later confided that "the church encourages its members to vote for the government party."

Like the traditional _patrão_, the _pastor presidente_ assumes the role of intermediary between his followers and the political power structure. Although he cannot force his political choices on the church membership, the _pastor presidente_ can exert a decisive influence on the way members of the Assembléia vote. This became quite evident during the 1974 elections when two members of the Assembléia ran for state deputy on the government party's (ARENA) electoral slate. In the weeks that preceded the election it became clear that church members wanted to know how the pastor would vote. The pastor, however, unwilling to alienate either of the two candidates, refused to divulge his choice, claiming that "both are good and honest men." This only increased the anxiety and speculations of church members. Church leaders and members of the pastor's family were constantly queried as to who the pastor would vote for or whether he had hinted that he preferred one candidate over the other.

The pastor's reticence did not mean that he or the church had little interest in the outcome of the election. Given the nature of Brazil's electoral system, each of the two legal parties (ARENA and MDB) divide the number of seats in the state legislature in accordance with the proportion of the total vote each receives. Thus, the parties seek a number of candidates who, while perhaps incapable of winning an election on their own, can draw in a large block of votes. As one former national deputy informed me, Brazil's political parties make a special effort to include at least one candidate from the Assembléia de Deus.[7] In the election described above, it made little difference which of the two Assembléia candidates received more votes. What mattered, of course, was the fact that since both men belonged to ARENA, the church's support would go to the government party. The propaganda employed by ARENA demonstrates the importance attached to mobilizing the Pentecostal vote. One handout distributed at Pentecostal churches described the candidate from the Assembléia as "the only Evangelical candidate who has served our people since 1963 as <u>vereador</u> (city councilman) in Recife and who has had the help of the Lord." By delivering a large number of votes to the party in power, the church gains access to government favors. It must be pointed out, however, that it is the pastor and not the candidate himself who plays a central role in these political maneuverings, for without his support candidates would find it impossible to mobilize the vote of the Assembléia. In the case of the 1974 election, for example, each of the candidates was careful to secure the pastor's approval before entering the race.

From this brief examination of Recife's Assembléia de Deus, it becomes apparent that many aspects of Brazil's traditional society have taken root and thrived in the Pentecostal sects. In this sense, the rapid growth of Pentecostalism does not represent a break, symbolic or otherwise, with the traditional social order. What then, is the relationship between the rapid growth of the Pentecostal movement and the socio-economic changes described at the beginning of this paper?

Rapid urbanization, industrial growth and the rationalization of export agriculture produced severe stresses and strains on traditional social relationships. The application of modern technology to plantation agriculture, especially in the sugar producing regions of Northeast Brazil, a process which began late in the 19th century, but accelerated rapidly after World War II, has displaced many peasants from the land, thereby helping to trigger a wave of rural to urban migrations that reached their peak during the decades of the 1950's and 1960's. Those who remained on the land no longer dealt with a traditional <u>patrão</u>, but with an impersonal administrator whose principle concerns were cutting costs and meeting production quotas. Disintegration of traditional relationships effected urban as well as rural dwellers.

An expanding urban population as well as the physical growth of the city itself, made it increasingly difficult to maintain traditional community relationships. As a result of both a shortage of Brazilian priests and a tradition of neglect when it came to dealing with the needs of the masses, the Catholic Church proved incapable of providing a basis for the restructuring of community life. Under these circumstances organizations like the Assembléia de Deus became increasingly attractive to rural and urban lower classes.[8] At a time when traditional social relationships are in the process of disintegration they offer their members the security of a community modeled upon familiar and comfortable patterns. Thus Pentecostalism can be viewed as a conservative force, one which tends to preserve and even strengthen the established forms of social organization.

NOTES

[1] These figures are based on estimates of Pentecostal growth made by Read (1967:184). The Brazilian census does not distinguish between the various Evangelical denominations. The Pentecostal community refers to those who attend church services but for one reason or another are not members. Most scholars use a ration of 2 to 2 1/2 individuals for every church member to figure the total church community. See, Read, 1965:184; Curry, 1968:19.

[2] Historic Protestant churches refers to the earliest Protestant denominations to evangelize in Brazil, such as the Presbyterians, Methodists, Baptists and Congregationalists.

[3] The German Luthern church is non-proselytic and almost entirely confines its members to German immigrants and their descendants.

[4] Figures based on the Estatística do Culto Protestante, 1968. Published for 12 years, this census was the only official accounting of Evangelical membership by denomination. It has not been published since 1969.

[5] Bryan Wilson (1961:1) speaks of the totalitarianism of the sect, which is not "only an ideological unit, it is to a greater or lesser extent, a social unit, seeking to enforce behavior on those who accept belief, and seeking every occasion to draw the faithful apart from the rest of society and into the company of each other."

[6] Pentecostals believe that the Holy Spirit may bless them with certain powers. The most common sign of having received power from the Spirit is the Baptism with the Holy Spirit. This occurs when the individual goes into a trance and speaks in tongues. At a minimum it implies a special communion with the Spirit. Other powers include faith healing, the power of discernment, the power of interpretation, the power of of persuasion, and the power to prophetize.

[7] Interview with Dr. Paulo F. do Rego Maciel, former Federal Deputy from Pernambuco.

[8] There do, of course, exist other available forms of organization such as the Spiritualist groups, the Afro-Brazilian cults, regional associations, and sports clubs. However, none of these seem to provide the same degree of community as Pentecostalism does.

REFERENCES CITED

Curry, Donald Edward
    1968   Lusíada: An Anthropological Study of the Growth of Protestantism in Brazil. Ann Arbor, University Microfilms.

Hutchinson, Bertram
    1966   "The Patron-Dependent Relationship in Brazil. A Preliminary Examination," *Sociologia Ruralis* 1:3-30.

Medina, J.
    1964   Consideraciones sociológicas sobre el desarrollo económico. Buenos Aires, Solar/Hachette.

Read, William R.
    1967   Fermento religioso nas massas do Brasil. São Paulo, Imprensa Metodista.

Willems, Emilio
    1964   "Protestantism and Culture Change in Brazil and Chile," in W. D'Antonio and F. Pike (eds.) Religion, Revolution and Reform. London, Burns & Oates.

    1967   Followers of the New Faith: Culture Change and the Rise of Protestantism in Brazil and Chile. Nashville, Vanderbilt University Press.

Wilson, Bryan
    1961   Sects and Society. London, Heinemann Publishers.

CAPITALISM AND RELIGION AT THE PERIPHERY:

PENTECOSTALISM AND UMBANDA IN BRAZIL.

GARY NIGEL HOWE

UNIVERSITY OF KANSAS

Consideration of how Pentecostalism is related to social change in Brazil requires both specification of the basic structural changes in the national polity and economy and, within the parameters of a symposium devoted to the relation between Pentecostalism and modernization in the Third World, evaluation of the extent to which these changes are adequately captured in the concept "modernization." In order to appreciate the full cognitive effects of these changes it will be necessary to go beyond scrutiny of Pentecostalism to analysis of other religious formations emerging in apparently the same circumstances in the national context. The general conclusion to be drawn is that Brazil is changing but not modernizing, and that within the context of the specific nature of the developments in polity and economy Pentecostalism, or Pentecostal-type religion, is very much the exception rather than the rule--even in those areas where the concept of modernity seems most applicable.

In commenting upon religious developments in Brazil I wish to emphasize not the associational life of the new religions, not the functions--both material and "spiritual"--of membership in Pentecostal congregations, but the nature of emergent cosmologies. More specifically, attention will be paid not to the relation between specific religio-ideological propositions and mundane interests (e.g., between world rejection and poverty) but to the most fundamental assumptions about the nature of divinity, society and the individual underpinning all religious statements within a specific religious "current." The aim is a classical one:

to establish a relation between the organization
of the relations between the constitutive elements
of religious cosmology and the structure of interaction in the mundane world. Somewhat different
from the exemplars of this approach (Durkheim,
1915; Durkheim and Mauss, 1970), however, is the
observation that in Brazil "society" finds its reflection not in a single representative religion
but in quite contradictory religious formulations.

The concept "modernization" constitutes a
major obstacle to appreciation of developments in
Brazil and, in all probability, in the Third World
as a whole. The Third World is not modernizing,
it is being integrated in a new way into the international capitalist economy--frequently on the
basis of the internal development of commodity production for national consumption and the widespread emergence of a free proletariat engaged for
the first time in the national political process.
It is relatively clear that modernization is a concept aggregating a series of institutional and
structural changes observed in connection with the
development of capitalism and nation states in
what is now the "advanced" world. However, it can
be argued that capitalist development in the Third
World--as radically conditioned by the existence
of the advanced sector of the world economy, past
and present relations to international markets, and
penetration by foreign capital (see Frank, 1971)--
does not and cannot reproduce the experience of
the advanced sector. The existence and action of
the advanced sector in the world economy specifically precludes the emergence in the Third World
of that Western institutional complex commonly
called the "modern" condition. The Third World is
changing, but is not necessarily reliving the social history of the advanced capitalist areas.
This is not to argue Third World exceptionalism,
but merely that the internal and external conditions of change in these areas are quite different from those experiences in Europe.

Of course, elements of the sociological notion of modernity are present and important in
Brazil, but these find their place and limitations
in a totality quite different from that to be an-

ticipated on the basis of a theoretical perspective viewing the whole as moving in a single "direction" in an integrated and coherent fashion. Just as "modernity" is present, so is Pentecostalism. But this, too, is but one element of a larger religious complex characterized by considerable heterogeneity of form as well as of substance. To characterize social change in Brazil as modernization, and to represent Pentecostalism as the major religious response to this process is a temptation to which some have succumbed (e.g., Willems, 1967), but only at the cost of ignoring the radical contradictions generated in both social life and thought by that process which is so misleadingly and disarmingly termed modernization, rather than what it truly is--the development and transformation of the hegemony of capital at the periphery.

At first glance, religious and social change in Brazil appear simply definable and harmoniously related. The development of a centralized and bureaucratic state structure from a loose federation, and the development of commodity production oriented toward a more or less unified national market from a situation of a mixture of semi-subsistence agriculture and rationalized export monoculture[1] seem to find their spiritual complement in the development of Pentecostalism, which by contrast with folk Catholicism in Brazil (Queiroz, 1968; Guimaraes, 1974), is characterized by the individualization of religious action (the personal responsibility of the believer), the consolidation of effective religious power in the hands of a unitary godhead (as opposed to the multiplicity of hierarchicalized and localized religious forces in folk Catholicism), and the objectification of a coercive and intrusive religious order articulated through universal rules (as opposed to the voluntarism and negotiated character of man-saint relations in Catholicism).[2] The individualization, rationalization, and increasingly compulsory character of relations in everyday life as engendered by both economic and political changes eroding personal and local autonomies reappear in the social construction of the religious life in a process which appears to be one of simple structural replication--where Religion reflects Society (Howe, 1977).

However, such a simple characterization of change, and such an unproblematic rendering of the relation between transformations at the practical and cognitive levels can only be achieved by restricting the sociological gaze to the most public and manifest symptoms of change. Looking outside of Pentecostalism--reviewing other new religions in Brazil, which may not demonstrate the same open and visible character as Pentecostalism--we are inevitably forced to concede that this is far from the sole response to change. Of particularly dramatic complexion is the development and growth of Umbanda parallel to Pentecostalism, a phenomenon which is even more located in the urban, industrial, and "modern" sectors of the national society, and which, perhaps, exerts an even greater ideological influence than Pentecostalism--for in spite of the "obvious" elective affinity of the latter religion for modernizing societies, it enjoys the consistent support of no more than four percent of the total population (Read, 1969). What is remarkable about this parallel development is not pluralism--for sociologists of religion are long accustomed to the phenomenon of a religious tradition being borne by a variety of institutionalized religious associations in complex societies--but the fact that these religions are contradictory at the most fundamental level of general representations about the nature of the religious cosmos (Fry and Howe, 1975).

Umbanda, unlike Pentecostalism and Protestantism in general in Brazil, is not of recent missionary origin. Rather, it seems to constitute a fusion of elements of Afro-Brazilian spirit possession cults carried by the slave population of Brazil and a French-inspired Spiritism (Brown, 1974; Pressel, 1973). The particular balance between these elements varies immensely from cult center to cult center, the significant point being that it is in no way a simple continuation of "traditional religions" but constitutes a flexible innovation--appearing in the 1930s--appropriating symbols from a variety of sources:

from Catholicism, from long-established Afro-Brazilian cults, and, it has been alleged, from Amerindian sources. It is a spirit possession religion in which communication between spiritual powers and men is established by the manifestation of the spirit in the body of a religious medium (when possessed or in "trance"). It is not a religion of worship and adoration: the relationship between man and spirit is established for specific and limited purposes, i.e., the enlistment of the aid of the spirit for mundane purposes, be this for the cure of disease or the attainment of social goals. In many ways this relationship can be conceived of as one established on the basis of exchange in which mundane and spiritual actors transfer services between themselves. To a degree, Umbanda, unlike Pentecostalism, is not a self-contained cosmological system. Most adepts identify themselves as Catholics for the purposes of official censuses--which may be partly explicable in terms of the rather stigmatized status of the religion, but which also reflects the complementarity of the two "religions" from the point of view of the umbandista. This complementarity should be understood as Catholicism's contribution of the notion of a high god which, however otiose, tempers the polytheistic emphasis encountered in the practice of Umbanda. The otiose nature of the high god is of particular significance. Its integration into the cosmology of the umbandista appears to reflect a belief in a coherent and unified order which, fortunately or not, does not seem to be decisive in structuring particular interactions, in which resort to manipulable and relatively amoral spiritual agents is certainly a more efficacious means of promoting worldly interests.

It is impossible here to fully elaborate upon the cosmology subjacent to the practice of Umbanda and the frequently subtle ways it differs from Pentecostalism. Instead, I will simply list some gross contradictions taking Pentecostalism as the contrast class. In Umbanda polytheism stands against monotheism; optional relations with spirits are opposed to obligatory relations; particularism contrasts with universalism; and the mediated nature of the religious relation is opposed to the direct relation with God.

In spite of frequent protestations by Brazilian sociologists (e.g., Camargo, 1973) to the effect that these religions are "functionally equivalent" (a formulation which considerably simplifies the problem of explanation), it is clear that they are ideologically opposed. They are equivalent in only one major dimension: both emphasize the good of the individual as opposed to that of society at large. But even here they differ. The umbandista might, with the help of the spirits, attain his personal good (defined in material this-worldly terms) within society; the Pentecostal can find good (defined in salvationist and spiritual terms) outside society, either in the bosom of the church or, more fully, in the heavenly praxis after death.

The development of both of these religions at the same time (largely from the 1930s) and within the same context would appear to constitute a serious anthropological and sociological embarrassment. We can easily cope with different social ethics generated out of different mundane social positions and interests, but such differences in basic assumptions about the nature of the religious cosmos present an altogether more radical problem with regard to "reflection" theories of the social grounding of religious beliefs and cognition in general. If modernization is really a coherent process, how can it give rise to contradictory representations? One possible answer is that it does not--that Umbanda represents a traditional rearguard action against the acme of modernity, i.e., Pentecostalism. Unfortunately, Umbanda is not recognizably traditional. On the one hand, Umbanda is clearly innovative in respect to traditional Afro-Brazilian cults--both in regard to cosmology and its bearing group (cf. Brown, 1976). Continuity with folk Catholicism appears a more promising proposition: this, too, was characterized by an effectively otiose high god, by a multiplicity of spiritual forces (saints etc.), by negotiation between man and saint, by the possibility of transient relations dominated by the idiom of exchange, and, apparently, by mediated religious relations. These similarities, however striking, prove to be somewhat superficial. The priest is not a permanently necessary intermediary in folk Catholicism. Religious action was not exclusively individualistic and this-worldly--salvationist aspects cannot be ignored, nor the fact that collectivities of various kinds frequently established joint relations with spiritual powers, a phenomenon not typical of Umbanda (an exception is the collective celebration of the cult of a particular spirit, e.g., the great festa de Iemanjá held on the beach at Santos. The significance of collective action in relation to this specific figure has yet to be adequately explicated). Furthermore, a major difference resides in the fact that Catholicism of the folk variety can be considered in part a cult of community. Religion sanctified and expressed the communal social order. This is definitely not the case in Umbanda--whose attraction precisely exists in the opportunities it offers to circumvent the "ideal" social order--an aspect which is undoubtedly contributory to its public stigmatization by the ideologists of social order (whatever these might practice in private) (Vergolino e Silva, 1976). Umbanda is not a direct continuation of traditional systems of practice and belief.

In short, it is clear that both Pentecostalism and Umbanda are innovative responses to recent social change--making any simple pronouncements about religious and social transformation singularly unenlightening. But if the religious change, upon close examination, appears somewhat ambiguous, so does the reality of "modernization" in itself appear less than convincing in Brazil. Here, in spite of a public rhetoric of legal-rational administration, of efficient production, and of the predominance of purely technical considerations in the organization of formal social action, patronage, nepotism, "back-scratching" and pork-barrel politicking thrive (Graham, 1968; Leeds, 1964)--along, that is, with more venal forms of corruption. We might ascribe all these practices to "tradition" again--but evidence exists to suggest that such practices have blossomed on such a large scale only in recent years, and that, furthermore, the organization of these relations does not exactly replicate that of the traditional patron-client relations of the interior. It would seem that parallel to the cognitive contradiction between Pentecostalism and Umbanda there is a social contradiction between legal-rational universalism and negotiated particularistic relations (Parsons, 1951). Furthermore, both the latter and Umbanda seem to be the product of precisely the process more obviously throwing up Pentecostalism and more impersonal bureaucratic organization, i.e., "modernization."

Clearly, in order to comprehend the internal contradiction we will have to pass to the concrete reality of change in Brazil. The recent phase of modernization in Brazil is not one of integration into the international capitalist economy. That particular linkage was created some centuries ago (Furtado, 1963; Wallerstein, 1974): the change we refer to is the emergence and growing hegemony of industrial capital oriented to the national economy as market. Nonetheless, an appreciation of the meaning of the previous export-dominated structure is essential for understanding the particular dynamics of the modern Brazilian situation --just as it is for an understanding of the political economy of many areas of the Third World. The previous orientation of capital to production for external markets produced: i) a high degree of internal economic segmentation; ii) a high degree of regionalism; iii) a weak and limited central state structure; and iv) a large population on the fringes of market production. The political order was oligarchic, and involved minimum mobilization of the mass of the population (Queiroz, 1969).

The crisis of the export economy in the 1930s acted to weaken the hegemony of export capital and provide some of the conditions for a bid for power on the part of the industrial capitalist class. That is, I am suggesting that from the 1930s there develops a substantial conflict within the capitalist class itself. This conflict essentially revolved around the construction and utilization of a strong central state organization. The export bourgeoisie had little interest in or use for a strong central state. The industrial bourgeoisie, on the other hand, required one for the rapid construction of the social overhead capital necessary for industrial and internal commercial expansion, and for the protection of native industry against competition presented by foreign producers, i.e., the industrial capitalists of the advanced sector of the world economy.

At this stage neither form of capital (or group) was capable of dominating the other on the basis of its own resources: the issue could only be decided by mobilizng other elements of the population which had hitherto constituted only peripheral elements of the political scene. From 1945 until 1964, when a new set of alliances emerged, the fate of the different capitals was to be decided in the political arena. Democracy was resorted to in order to mobilize forces sufficient to decide the issue.

While these struggles may appear either too "high level" or too banal to account for contradictions in the organization of everyday social life, this is in fact not the case. Let us remember: industrial capital was striving for the creation of a strong bureaucratic state; it sought to establish a regime of rationalized capital investment; it sought to create a truly national economy; and it sought to order the existence of the mass of the population--as citizens and wage laborers--within the parameters of centralized, bureaucratic institutions. In the advanced capitalist world these were the essential conditions for modernization and the emergence of the sort of rationalized monotheism such as, I suggest, Pentecostalism represents in Brazil. "Modernization" was clearly linked to the fate of the industrial bourgeoisie. In the event, these interests did win out in Brazil--but only by resort to forms of mobilization which undermined the very "modern" relations which the bourgeois state and industrial capital typically carried with them in the history of the West.

Put in the simple terms necessitated by limitations of space, the mobilization of the mass of the population in support of any policy of national scope required resort to patronage on an immense and quite unprecedented scale. This was conditioned by the prior hegemony of export capital: one, the resort to mass mobilization was necessitated by the opposition presented by the export bourgeoisie; and two, the national segmentation derivative from the export orientation precluded resort to coherent national programs in order to gain support. Broad class appeals were insufficient because, in Brazil's mosaic, there were no broad national classes. The effects of this upon political organization were remarkable: on the one hand, all the parties searching to create alliances between diverse social interests were constrained to create programs which could alienate practically no one--hence the emergence of "nationalisms" and "populisms" appealing to the interests of the people or nation as a whole--this line being replete with calls for the rationalization and modernization of administration and the economy; on the other hand, the very ambiguity and generality of these programs led parties to attempt to consolidate support on a much more materialistic and particularistic basis--i.e., the distribution of spoils (cf. Anderson and Cockroft, 1966). Such a phenomenon should be viewed against the background of the enormous influence of the state--both direct and indirect--in the economy. The necessities of support mobilization involved the factual distribution of resources on the basis not of legal-rational criteria but on the basis of political favors (Cardoso, 1972). Pyramids of brokerage developed--with quite extra-legal favors being granted by intermediaries to political supporters in exchange for votes. Personal clientship rather than impersonal citizenship became the most significant dimension of political being --and political being was a major dimension in the general determination of life chances.

It is relatively clear that this emergent system of mediated, personalistic, and frequently extra-legal exchanges is the social basis for the cognitive legitimacy of Umbanda. The spiritual system at one and the same time reflected and expanded the mundane system of interaction and resource distribution. The general structure emergent with the rise to power on the part of industrial capital and its state organization was beset by contradictions: on the one hand, these interests strove to create rationalized and centralized structures of interaction; on the other hand, in order to gain power they had to resort to a relatively decentralized, personalistic patronage system (Pinto, 1969). The internal contradiction is not one of tradition versus modernity, but one inherent in the development of industrial capital in the context of previous national economic dependence.

What is remarkable in this context is not Umbanda but the existence of Pentecostalism. That which seems most representative of modernization breathes rather thin air in this situation of widespread patronage because change in Brazil does not involve modernization as we ethnocentrically define it. Truly, apparently modern institutions emerge, e.g., the centralized formally and rhetorically legal-rational state. However, the real organization and meaning of these forms is not intrinsic but shaped by the dominant problematic of the leading social forces of the time. The meaning of the particular is embedded in the organization of the totality, which is quite different from that defining the meaning and impact of similar institutions in the European context.

In this situation it comes as no surprise that the penetration of Pentecostalism should be so limited. Pentecostals exist not because they are near the forces of modernization but precisely because they are so marginal to normal social existence. Patronage tends to flow through pre-established social networks such as the extended family. Pentecostals in Brazil, in contrast to umbandistas, appear to be exactly those whose extended family networks have disintegrated and who are newcomers to the cities. They are those not inserted into patronage networks and whose religious commitments preclude the development of stable linkages to such informal organizations: they are Pentecostals because they have an exceptional life experience. Without patronage they do, indeed, confront the ideal legal-rational structure. Getulio Vargas once said: "To our friends everything, to our enemies the law." Without patrons the Pentecostals have the law--and, in consequence, a peculiarly "modern" vision based on a quite atypical social existence. In relation to the organization of the society around them the Pentecostals modernized not wisely but too well.

In conclusion, my title indicates that my comments on social and religious change have an application wider than the specific case of Brazil. However, I am not suggesting that the Brazilian situation must necessarily be reproduced throughout the periphery or Third World. It is not inevitable that a powerful central state relying upon the mobilization of popular support for its very existence should be generated from the conflict between export agriculture and internally oriented industry. What is characteristic of central state formation in the Third World is not necessarily a common <u>etiology</u> but a common predicament--i.e., the centralized states develop prior to national classes and "nations." What is more, these states tend to be rather significant economic forces. Given the relative paucity of native private capital and the need for promotion of internal industry and export sectors, the state does not merely police the ring for private capital but intervenes directly in the economy--a large part of the resources of which it directly or indirectly controls. The state emerges as an attractive prize in the national arena, but there are no national groups capable of dominating it alone--a situation at least partially conditioned by the previous penetration of export capital fostering internal economic segmentation. What we consistently find in these situations is corruption, pork-barrel politics and particularism: the mobilization of support not on the basis of policy interests in common (which could only spring from truly national interest groups) but on the basis of spoils--be this seen as distribution of the resources controlled by the state or by differential application of law--irrespective of the formal rationalizing interests of those involved in commodity production or constructing the central state apparatus. The political necessities of mobilizing political support constantly undermine the legal-rational polity and institute a patrimonial regime whose inner organization specifically contradicts diacritical features of modernity.

The general issue at stake here is the way in which we conceive of modernization. If we cling to its strict sense in sociological typologizing there is no real possibility of understanding developments in the Third World nor of understanding the significance of Pentecostalism within it. The development of the nation-state and commodity production does not have the same social meaning in the periphery as in the historic core. The class fragmentation of the periphery, the low volume of internal trade, the importance of the state for the economic life of the nation, all conspire to produce agitated polities dominated not by national classes with clearly articulated common interests but by shifting and eclectic coalitions held together by the discriminatory and particularistic distribution of public resources. In this context we can hardly expect patterns of social interaction equivalent to those in Western Europe, which developed under quite different internal and external conditions. Mauss (1954) remarked that the circulation of goods in acephalous societies was profoundly conditioned by the polity--that the public circulation of goods was almost a modality of the political life. I suggest that this has no small relevance for social organization at the periphery: irrespective of narrow economic interest in exchange and circulation, the conditions for political survival must be met. Life is not split into political and economic "spheres," for the two merge in practice in a process of internal development in which "modernity" and Pentecostal type formations are not the rule, but very much the exception.

Footnotes

1. The totality and coherence of these changes have rarely been discussed. For elements of rural change see Caldeira (1956), Pierson (1966), Candido (1964) and Shirley (1971). Aspects of central state formation and organization are discussed by Balan et al. (1974), Graham (1968), and Brasileiro (1973). An essential work for understanding "traditional" organization is Leal (1975).

2. We follow Leonard (1953) in emphasizing Pentecostalism's radical continuity with more traditional Protestantisms. This can be justified by the structural nature of the analysis. Equally important, however, is the observation that "charismatic" gifts appear to be more important ideologically than practically in many Brazilian Pentecostal churches.

Bibliography

Anderson, Bo and James D. Cockroft
1966   "Control and co-optation in Mexican politics," International Journal of Comparative Sociology, 7:1, pp. 219-244.

Balan, Jorge (org.)
1974   Centro e periferia no desenvolvimento brasileiro. São Paulo, DIFEL.

Brasileiro, Ana Maria
1973   O município como sistema político. Rio de Janeiro, FGV.

Brown, Diana
1974   "Political aspects of Umbanda, an indigenous urban religion in Brazil," ms. Annual Meeting of Latin American Studies Association, San Francisco.

1976   "O papel histórico da classe média na

Umbanda," ms. Tenth Congress of Associação Brasileira de Antropologia, Salvador, Bahia.

Caldeira, C.
1956 Mutirão: formas de ajuda mútua no meio rural. São Paulo, Nacional.

Camrago, C. P. F. de
1973 Católicos, Protestantes, Espíritas. Petropolis, Vozes.

Candido, A.
1964 Os parceiros do Rio Bonito. Rio de Janeiro, José Olympio.

Cardoso, F. H.
1972 Empresário industrial e desenvolvimento econômico no Brasil. São Paulo, DIFEL.

Durkheim, E.
1915 The elementary forms of the religious life. London, Allen & Unwin.

Durkheim, E. and M. Mauss
1970 Primitive classification. London, Routledge.

Frank, A. G.
1971 Capitalism and underdevelopment in Latin America. Harmondsworth, Penguin.

Fry, P. H. and G. N. Howe
1975 "Duas respôstas a aflição: Umbanda e Pentecostalismo," Debate e Crítica, no. 6, pp. 49-74.

Furtado, C.
1963 The economic growth of Brazil. Berkeley, University of California Press.

Graham, L. S.
1968 Civil Service Reform in Brazil. Austin, University of Texas Press.

Guimaraes, A. M. Z.
1974 Os homens de deus: um estudo compara-

tivo sobre o sistema de crenças e práticas do catolicismo em algumas áreas do Brasil rural. Rio de Janeiro, M.A. thesis, Museu Nacional.

Howe, G. N.
1977 "Representações religiosas e capitalismo: uma 'leitura' estruturalista," Cadernos do ISER, no. 6, pp. 39-48.

Leal, V. N.
1975 Coronelismo, enxada e voto: o município e o regime representativo. São Paulo, Alfa-Omega.

Leeds, A.
1964 "Brazilian careers and social structure: an evolutionary model and case history," American Anthropologist, 66: 6, pp. 1321-1347.

Leonard, E. G.
1953 L'illuminisme dans un protestantisme de constitution récente (Brésil). Paris, Presses Universitaires de France.

Mauss, M.
1954 The Gift. New York, Free Press.

Parsons, T.
1951 The Social System. New York, Free Press.

Pierson, D.
1966 Cruz das Almas. Rio de Janeiro, José Olympio.

Pinto, R. S.
1969 The political ecology of the Brazilian Bank for Development (BNDE). Washington, O.A.S.

Pressel, E.
1973 "Umbanda in São Paulo: religious innovation in a developing society," in Erika Bourguignon (ed.), Religion, Altered States of Consciousness, and

Social Change. Columbus, Ohio State
University Press.

Queiroz, M. I. P. de
1968   "O catolicismo rústico no Brasil,"
             Revista do Instituto de Estudos Bra-
             sileiros, no. 5.

1969   O mandonismo local na vida política
             brasileira. São Paulo, Instituto de
             Estudos Brasileiros.

Read, W. R.
1969   Latin America Church Growth. Grand
             Rapids, Eerdmans.

Shirley, R. W.
1971   The end of a tradition. New York,
             Columbia University Press.

Vergolino e Silva, A.
1976   O tambor das flores. Campinas, UNICAMP,
             M.A. thesis in Social Anthropology.

Wallerstein, E.
1974   The modern world system. New York,
             Academic Press.

Willems, E.
1967   Followers of the New Faith. Nashville,
             Vanderbilt University Press.

Catholic Pentecostalism: A New Word
in the New World

Thomas J. Chordas
Duke University

The purpose of this paper is fourfold: to give examples of the expansion in Latin America of an Anglo-American religious movement, 'Catholic Pentecostalism' or the 'Catholic Charismatic Renewal'; to assess the potential impact of the movement within the Roman Catholic Church in Latin America; to suggest the fruitfulness of a class-based comparison between Catholic Pentecostalism and the older so-called 'classical Pentecostalism'; and to outline some theoretical problems in the study of Pentecostalism as a social and religious phenomenon.[1]

The Charismatic Renewal synthesizes elements of Pentecostalism, such as Baptism in the Holy Spirit and 'spiritual gifts' or $charism_a$, with Catholic sacramental and liturgical forms. The central ritual event for Catholic Pentecostals is a weekly prayer meeting. Other common ritual practices are initiation of new members and healing through prayer. The movement aims at a personal transformation of its participants and a general renewal of Church life. Catholic Pentecostal groups are of various sizes and exhibit varying degrees of commitment among members. In sum, the movement can be characterized as communitarian, enthusiastic, healing-oriented, and revitalistic.

The Catholic Charismatic Renewal originated in the United States in 1967. Before that time Catholics who underwent the Pentecostal experience typically left the Church, rejecting Catholicism as incompatible with their new faith. The movement had its initial popularity in Catholic universities, but soon spread to the wider Catholic public in parishes across the country. Contrary to the common conception that Pentecostalism is a working class religion, many Catholic Pentecostals were well-educated middle-class people (cf. Mawn,

1975; Séguy, 1976). The movement began to spread abroad around 1970. By 1977 the <u>International Directory</u> of Catholic charismatic prayer groups, claiming not to be comprehensive, listed 3,000 groups in the United States and Canada, and 1,600 in 82 other countries.[2] Accurate membership statistics are not available, but an educated guess would be that there are today as many as 500,000 Catholic Pentecostals.

Catholic Latin America was the first and most likely arena for Catholic Pentecostal expansion;[3] only after autumn 1976 do reports from the rest of the world begin to outnumber those from this region. Official endorsement of the movement was announced by the Annual Caribbean Conference of Catholic Bishops in 1975, in a joint statement by a Chilean cardinal and bishop late in 1976, by the Antilles Episcopal Conference at the new year of 1977 (recognition of the entire movement was given by Pope Paul VI in the summer of 1975 at the international Catholic Pentecostal conference in Rome). Catholic bishops who have been Baptized in the Holy Spirit number at least half a dozen in this predominantly lay movement, and preside in Haiti, Colombia, Guatemala, Honduras, Venezuela (an archbishop), and Brazil. The movement is at present more developed in northern Latin America and the Caribbean than in the south (with the exception of Chile). Attempts have been made to coordinate activities at national levels by establishing 'service committees' and/or 'communications offices' in most of these countries. Since 1971 the movement has held an annual Latin American Catholic Charismatic Leaders' Conference (ECCLA). In 1976, ECCLA IV attracted over three hundred leaders, plus the participation of eight bishops.[4] In 1977 at Caracas, ECCLA V attracted 160 leaders from twenty-two countries, plus Spanish-speaking delegates from the USA, Canada, Spain, and the Canary Islands (at least three bishops were also present). Information on specific instances of the movement's development is available from the Caribbean, from Mexico, and from Chile.[5]

The Caribbean

The movement was introduced into the Caribbean in 1971. As in most areas of the Third World, the initial impetus came from missionaries with 'charismatic' contacts in the United States (or Canada). By 1975 there were more than 150 Catholic Pentecostal 'prayer groups' in the region; the distribution of groups and members among the various islands is depicted in Table 1.

Table 1

Estimate of Total Participation in the Caribbean as of November, 1975

Country	Number of Prayer Groups	Persons Involved
Barbados	4	150
Belize	8	600
Dominica	2	20
Grenada and Genadines	25	1,000
Guyana	8	400
Jamaica	10	500
St. Lucia	2	200
St. Vincent	3	100
Trinidad and Tobago	55	4,000

(Source: *ICO Newsletter* Jan. 1976).

Dominican Republic	990	25,000

(As of Jan., 1978. Source ICO Newsletter, May, 1978.)

A rough estimate would put the number of participants in Haiti (where the movement began among Carmelite nuns in Cap-Haitien) at 600. Figures for Puerto Rico are unavailable, but would doubtless be in the same range as those for the Dominican Republic.

A Caribbean leadership conference in January of 1976 on Trinidad drew 120 delegates from fourteen islands and nations, and included the participation of the Archbishop of Trinidad: a similar conference in 1977 drew 200 delegates and included the participation of bishops from Jamaica, Trinidad and Grenada. A group in Puerto Rico sponsors periodic conferences and publishes a magazine (<u>Alabaré</u>) that circulates throughout Latin America.

The most important Catholic Pentecostal development in the Caribbean has occurred in a small town in Puerto Rico. The <u>municipio</u> of Aguas Buenas lies in the hills twelve miles south of San Juan and five miles west of Caguas. According to data from the US Census, <u>puebla</u> population in 1970 was 3,426, while total population including the outlying <u>barrios</u> amounted to 18,600. From 1960 to 1970 population in the town grew 9.2%, whereas the rural population declined 10.9% of the town population, 16.1% were born in the USA, nearly 10% higher than the national average. For the <u>municipio</u> as a whole 54.9% are rural non-farm residents and 26.7% are rural farm residents. Occupationally, 30.3% are engaged in manufacture, 19.6% are white collar, and 15.3% are government workers.[6] The parish church in Aguas Buenas is supplemented by ten small chapels in the surrounding <u>barrios</u>. Two small Pentecostal, and one small Baptist church (each about the size of one of the Catholic chapels) represent Protestantism in the <u>municipio</u>. Despite the recent popularity of Pentecostalism among the Catholics, there is little or no apparent contact between them and the classical Pentecostal churches.

The strong presence of Catholic Pentecostalism is closely related to the missionary status of the Catholic parish, whose four Redemptrist priests have contacts far beyond the immediate locality - two are from the USA (specifically, Brooklyn), one is an Argentinian, and one a Venezuelan. Since 1971 all four, plus all the nuns in the parish, have received the Baptism in the Holy Spirit. The local community has followed suit; of the nearly 20,000 total population, 10,000 reportedly attend church regularly, and between three and four thousand have been Baptized in the Holy Spirit.[7]

The parish priests are assisted in activities such as Baptisms, catechetics, and paraliturgical functions by eighteen lay 'Eucharistic ministers', all but one of whom has become a Catholic Pentecostal. Eighteen more were expected to be added at the time of research (though advisors from The Word of God suggested that effort be directed to further training of the original group). With the added dimension of parish life introduced by the new movement, a third group of eighteen leaders has emerged, each responsible for a 'district' within the nascent Catholic Pentecostal community (only a few of these men simultaneously serve as Eucharistic ministers). Since members of both parish elite groups have received the Baptism in the Holy Spirit, there is probably little rivalry; my informant (a leader of The Word of God) reports that there is little resistance to the movement in general since both lay and priestly power in the parish are held by Catholic Pentecostals.

Puerto Rico is commonly understood as half Latin and half Anglo-American. It has been said, however, that "If Puerto Rico is a bridge between two cultures, it is a bridge with three lanes going in one direction and only one in the other" (quoted in Christopulos, 1974:151). This metaphor is appropriate with respect to Catholic Pentecostalism, for although it is the most influential group in Latin America, Aguas Buenas is under the direct tutelage of the leading Catholic Pentecostalism community in the United States ("The Word of God" from Ann Arbor, Michigan). The manner in which alien cultural forms are finding a place here is indicated by developments under Anglo-American tutelage. Since the summer of 1976 the express goal has been to transform the Aguas Buenas parish into a 'covenant community' that embraces the entire population. Such a community is a highly committed, strictly disciplined, and hierarchically organized group based on a "covenant", or document specifying the terms of a solemn agreement. To assist in the process a leader from The Word of God and the members of his 'household'[8] were temporarily relocated in the Puerto Rican town.

Conversion and initiation to the group occurs in a 'Life in the Spirit Seminar'. In the United States the Seminar consists of seven weekly meetings, but in Aguas Buenas it is compressed into a two-day retreat (a pattern similar to that of los Cursillos de Cristianidad). Leaders regard this as a potent approach which generates such enthusiasm, which then must be consolidated in individuals by 'followup' retreats.

Group leaders have emphasized the development of male participation and leadership. The first retreat specifically for male members (on the subject of family life) was held in 1976. Six hundred men participated, representing nearly one-fourth of the municipio's population. In October a conversion retreat for men only emphasized the family, holiness, and being a 'man of God'. This emphasis is significant in light of the fact that while all the parish's Eucharistic Ministers are men, half of the Catholic Pentecostal leaders are women. The Americans' interest in changing this situation seems to reflect not so much a transformation of Latin machismo as an effort to convince men that male dominance can be appropriately expressed in the 'womanly' religious sphere; thus eliminating a potential arena of influence for women in Aguas Buenas.

Early in 1977 a system of 'discipling' or 'spiritual headship' was instituted. Two of the priests have entered headship relations with nine men of the parish. These men in turn have each begun 'to disciple' two or three others. This system provides spiritual advisors for individuals, while simultaneously establishing a hierarchical structure of authority based on intimate interpersonal relationships. In addition, the headship system is a useful framework for the cultivation of an elite cadre of leaders.

On the other hand, some basic cultural incompatibilities may prevent adoption by Puerto Ricans of the Catholic Pentecostal 'household' or the formal 'covenant' commitment without modification. The Anglo-American 'household' is essentially a reaction against the isolation of nuclear family living, and an attempt to replace it by fictive kinship within the 'family' formed by the religious community. In contrast, the commitments of the Puerto Rican extended family or parentesco (La Ruffa, 1971:28-29) extend beyond the boundaries of the religious group, and their reaction to the covenant 'household' is that it is an impropriety to "have strangers in your house." Formal covenant may come to be accepted with increased 'maturity' of the group and increasing acceptance of charismaties by other parishioners ("few pastors have the guts to let everyone not interested leave", comments one of The Word of God advisors). However, some feel that the rigorous discipline instituted by a covenant is unsuited to the Latin American temperament. More pragmatically, essential to the Catholic Pentecostal notion of 'covenant' are periodic ritual assemblies of the entire community; in Aguas Buenas only towns-people can manage to attend the weekly gatherings, and in any case there is no local building large enough to accommodate the entire group.

The weekly prayer meeting is without doubt the central ritual occasion for all Catholic Pentecostals. A Word of God advisor reports that meetings in Aguas Buenas are characterized by fiery preaching ("very Latin American in style"), loud and fast singing (it is "more melodious and sophisticated" at The Word of God); but there is little mature teaching or prophetic utterance ("spiritual gifts" are not well developed in these respects), or faith-healing and deliverance from evil spirits (techniques which are spiritually more "advanced"). There is no evidence as to whether these meetings are complemented by a reinterpretation of traditional Puerto Rican family rituals. These include the rosario, a nightlong religious party featuring folk music, refreshments, and recital of the rosary, and the <u>velorio</u>, a nine-night wake at which the rosary is recited in honor of the deceased (Fenton, 1969:216). Worthwhile study could be undertaken of Catholic Pentecostal treatment of these and other practices of folk Catholicism associated with the saints, who are seldom invoked by North American Catholic Pentecostals. Even more interesting is the potential articulation of Catholic Pentecostal faith-healing, 'deliverance' from evil spirits, and 'inner healing' of emotional problems with Puerto Rican spiritualism and witchcraft (<u>brujeria</u>). These traditional practices are considered to be outside the domain of Catholicism; but Le Ruffa (1971:80-81) describes a reluctant spiritualist who could probably quite easily shift the idiom of her work to the parallel language of Catholic Pentecostalism.

Mexico

The initiation of Catholic Pentecostalism in Mexico is attributed to the American Missionaries of the Holy Spirit. In June, 1971, Mexico City had one prayer group of forty members; by September, 1975, it was estimated that more than ten thousand Mexicans had become part of the movement. The Catholic Pentecostal directory lists groups in Chihuahua, Durango, Tijuana, and five in Mexico City (many more small groups must exist unreported). A Catholic Pentecostal conference in Mexico City in 1975 drew 3,500 participants representing twenty regions.

One of the most common sources of ambivalence among Catholic Pentecostals is the necessity of commitment to 'social action'. Anglo-American leaders recognize that their Latin American counterparts have taken a greater intitiative in this area than they have themselves. Nonetheless, the call to social commitment does not take an overt political form, but quickly becomes reduced to the traditional least common denominator of "helping the poor". To date, the examples most publicized in movement forums come from Mexico.

A group called <u>Justicia y Alabanza</u> (Justice and Praise), based at the Social Secretariat of the Archdiocese of Mexico City, initiated the first development in Ciudad del Lago, a squatter settlement adjacent to Mexico City's airport.[9] Population growth in this area has been particularly rapid: from 1960 to 1970 the municipality directly east of the airport grew from sixty thousand to six hundred thousand people (Cornelius, 1973:13). In 1972, two years after this particular settlement appeared, a group from the Social Secretariat established a Catholic Pentecostal prayer group. A resident factory worker was recruited as leader, the Life in the Spirit Seminar was introduced, and instruction about Catholic Pentecostalism was made available.

The pentecostal experience is credited with important motivational change in both groups involved. The middle-class organizers came to conceive their task as radical conversion to Christ rather than in terms of well-meaning 'concern for the poor'. The squatters began to abandon an individualistic materialism which emulates the middle class for an increasing communitarianism and pride of status. In consequence the Ciudad del Lago group has developed communal patterns of authority and decision-making, avoiding one-man leadership. Patterns of labor exchange have been established among prayer group members. A women's group knits and sells clothing as the basis of a common fund for emergencies, loans to the most needy, and wholesale food purchase. Families take turns in preparing a communal Sunday meal.

The attitude of middle class Catholic Pentecostals toward the poor extends beyond an emphasis on conversion. With backing in the form of legal advice, architectural planning, and financing, the squatters have gained legal title to land in Ciudad del Lago. They have made a proposal to build individual family dwellings, but have decided against individual ownership of lots. They share a common dining room, kitchen, garden, children's recreation center, and workshops. Non-Catholic Pentecostal residents who at first accused the group of "selling the squatters' interests" have since asked to join.

The combination of religious motivation and middle class patronage has also affected the squatters' attitudes toward civil authority. When police came to search for illegal building materials or lawyers came to order them off the land, the people began to greet them with hospitality rather than anger or fear. Whereas their early communications with authorities were characterized by submission and flattery, more recently they have demanded recognition as right-bearing citizens. In the process of efforts to organize, the group has resisted a government attempt to resettle which would have required the group to break up and move to different parts of the city (Talavera, 1976: 4-8).

A similar situation has arisen among squatters at the municipal dump in the border city of Juarez, which in 1969 had a total of thirty-eight squatter settlements (Ugalde, 1974).[10] Several local social workers were converted to Catholic Pentecostalism. Then in 1972 a middle class Catholic Pentecostal group from across the border in El Paso brought eight carloads of groceries and people for a Christmas dinner with "the poorest people they knew." The contact initiated by this event eventually led to reconciliation between two factions of peperiadores (scavengers) at the dump, who subsequently organized their trash industry into a profit-sharing cooperative. Following a 1975 crisis in which the dump manager refused to pay for sorted and collected trash, the governor ceded the dump's management and income to the people who live there. In this enterprise they receive assistance from middle-class Catholic Pentecostals in the form of administrative work, location of markets, and investigation of importation procedures (Talavera, 1976:4-8).

Chile

Catholic Pentecostalism was introduced to Chile in 1972 by Maryknoll and Holy Cross missionary fathers from the United States. At present there are at least sixty prayer groups in Santiago, three or four of which have memberships as large as 300-500 people. Prayer groups are based in parishes, though they are not official parish functions - as is often the case in the United States, many rectors tolerate but do not participate in the groups. Group composition is estimated to include fairly equal proportions of men and women (60% women was one leader's guess), and a high proportion of young people in their early twenties. Middle class groups account for about a third of the total number, while two thirds of the groups are located in poor neighborhoods. Among the latter is a nascent 'covenant community', headed by an Irish Columban missionary. The group is located in Manuel Rodriguez, a government sponsored resettlement project initiated in 1969.[11]

Local leadership in the Santiago area has de facto responsibility for a recently established National Service Committee, among whose activities is publication of a monthly magazine for the movement in Chile. Foremost among leaders are a Chilean Jesuit who is a former university rector, and the Irish Columban father who leads the fledgling community in Manuel Rodriguez. Another priest is well known for his expertise in deliverance from evil spirits. The Chilean hierarchy's first official response to Catholic Pentecostalism came in August, 1976, in pastoral letters by the Cardinal at Santiago and the Bishop of Aysen.[12] In October of the same year a national leaders' conference in Santiago was attended by 100 leaders from Santiago, 100 from elsewhere in Chile, and 25 from Argentina, Brazil, Paraguay, and Peru. This conference was a forum for two emissaries from The Word of God community to spread their ideas concerning proper group leadership, the discipline of everyday activities, healing, prophecy, and the development of covenant communities.

Elsewhere in Chile, the movement has been established in at least three areas: the provinces of Aysén and Atacama, and the Mapuche Indian region around Cholchol. In the isolated southern province of Aysén, it began in 1975. In a retreat conducted in 1976 by leaders from Santiago, the local bishop received the Baptism in the Spirit, and has since become a leading national proponent of the movement. In the equally isolated northern province of Atacama, a group was begun in 1973 at the mining town of Copiapó. Late that year, in the midst of the military coup against the Chilean government, leaders from Santiago arrived to conduct a Catholic Pentecostal retreat.

From the outset this Copiapó group hoped to develop a Christian community along the lines of the primitive church. The critical year for realizing this project was 1976. A permit was obtained from the military junta to hold meetings in six private homes (the right of assembly has been strictly curtailed since the coup - religious meetings may be held only in churches, chapels, or by special permit). Group organization was formalized: an 'Elders Group' of eight lay people was formed under the guidance of the pastor; an 'evangelization ministry' of fifteen people was formed; and members of a 'healing ministry' now perform monthly sessions of ritual healing, using techniques learned at retreats and workshops in Santiago. In 1976, six delegates from Copiapó attended the leaders' conference led by The Word of God emissaries. Their influence prompted the group to adopt a covenant community orientation. The collective name 'God is Love' was adopted, and a number of members made a formal commitment to the community.

Some of the Catholic Pentecostals originally felt a conflict of interests with membership in other parish organizations. The 'orthodox' Catholic Pentecostal attitude prevailed, however, and these people became convinced that the movement is not a separate organization, but is meant for the entire Church. In fact the group has apparently come to dominate much activity in the parish, including family catechesis, baptismal preparation, parish finances, and maintenance of the rectory. On the diocesan level, the group has identified itself with the bishop's call for renewal of the local church. At his request the 'evangelization ministry' worked for three months in two neighborhoods. In addition, the group has spread Catholic Pentecostal notions to the nearby towns of Vellemar, La Serena, Ovalle, Illapal, and Salamanca.

A development of quite a different sort was signalled by a Catholic Pentecostal retreat among the Mapuche Indians at Cholchol in July, 1975. The activities were led by emissaries from Santiago, with assistance from missionaries experienced with the Mapuche. Participants included sixty men and fifty women, from fifteen Mapuche communities; many of these were prominent people in their respective localities. A description of the reatreat by its leader is the only available account of Catholic Pentecostal ritual in Latin America. It is discussed in detail here for its value in showing the interplay of Catholic, Mapuche, and Pentecostal ritual forms. It also illustrates the age-old Catholic missionary practice (at least since Pope Gregory the Great) of assimilating indigenous religions to the Universal Church:

> On the first night of the retreat, the deep fervor of the Mapuche was evident from their attention, their reverence, their songs, and their hands raised in praise. I ventured to propose that we all praise God in a loud voice and the response was overwhelming.
> We incorporated various customs of the region into the retreat. In the seating we followed the Mapuche custom of women sitting in the front and men in back.[13] Two 'sargants' were nominated to direct the order of the proceedings (e.g., during the Mass) and

they did so with great responsibility, just as they do for Mapuche ceremonies. In praying for deliverance [from evil spirits] during the renewal of our baptismal promises, we adopted the naitún, or dance of prayer. While the Machi [Mapuche shamaness] played the cultrún drum and sang, we danced to and fro, varying our steps.[14] Then the four priests sprinkled those present with holy water. During the Mass, thirteen adults were baptized, and for the exorcism ceremony we adapted the use of the machitún (or healing) in which evil spirits are expelled to the accompaniment of knife movements and blows of the drum. We prayed over people to be baptized in the Spirit in four groups, two of men and two of women, because the Mapuche make great use of the number four in their ceremonies. It symbolizes totality.[15] Each group began with a purún (dance) to the acclamations of all those present. Then each group knelt to pray for a moment. They sang "Divine Spirit, descend", and the priests laid hands on their heads and prayed for each person in the group.

That night was a joyful one. There were Mapuche jests, games, and dances, such as the choique, in which the men imitate the flight of birds.

(Aldunate, 1975).

The organization of these events, far from being arbitrary, corresponds to that of the traditional Mapuche fertility rite, or nillatún (Faron, 1964). Participants in the nillatún are drawn from a group of Mapuche reservations linked by ritual and affinal ties and forming a 'ritual congregation' - it is likely that the fifteen localities represented at the Catholic Pentecostal retreat belong to such a ritual congregation. The purpose of nillatún is twofold: propitiation of ancestral spirits and nenechén, the Mapuche supreme deity; 2) dispersion of evil spirits from the ceremonial field. The principle events in the two-day ritual include the driving out of evil spirits (awn), ritual dance, a long oration in unintelligible secret language by the officiating priest (nillatufe), and the sacrifice of sheep. In the Catholic Pentecostal retreat these events are duplicated by deliverance, exorcism, and the sacrifice of the Mass; the substantial additions are the gestures of Christian commitment in Catholic Baptism and Pentecostal Baptism in the Holy Spirit.

The ethnographer of the Mapuche states that participation in nillatún by machi, who specialize in direct contact with the spirit world, has probably come about only recently due to a decline in the number of competent nillatufe, the Mapuche priests who specialize in ritual knowledge (Faron, 1964:105). The beneficent machi is further distinguished from the malevolent kalku or sorcerer. Her inclusion in the retreat takes advantage of her prestige and ability to treat themes of common interest to Mapuche and Catholic Pentecostal, namely evil spirits and healing.

Incorporation of the machitún ritual invokes another aspect of Mapuche religious practice, one that exists in a relation of fruitful ambiguity vis-à-vis pentecostal practice: in this ceremony the machi receives unintelligible messages ('prophecy in tongues') which are conveyed to the other participants ('interpreted') by a ritual assistant called thungumachin, and exercises the power ('spiritual gift') of healing. Traditionally, however, her prophecy and healing occur during a trance in which she communes with familiar spirits (pillan), a practice which would be regarded by pentecostals as inspired by Satan. The 'adaptation' of the ritual for this occasion undoubtedly eliminated the role of pillan.[16]

The ritual plot thickens in consideration of d'Epinay's (1969) discussion of classical Pente-

costal congregations in the Mapuche region
(d'Epinay refers specifically to the town of
Cholchol). Here, in contrast to the rest of
Chile, the sexual division of ritual labor
strictly parallels that of traditional Mapuche
society: men are pastors (<u>caciques</u>) and women
are prophetesses (<u>machis</u>). Further, prophecy in
tongues abounds in this region, and prophetesses
are especially responsible for the pantomimed
'ritual operations' performed in cases of serious
illness (d'Epinay, 1969:200-03). The comparison
between the two pentecostalisms is evident: while
classical Pentecostalism develops a separate, exclusive ritual organization that remains analogous
to the indigenous model, Catholic Pentecostalism
assimilates the indigenous model to its organization; the former converts Indians, the latter converts Indian culture. Catholic Pentecostalism
attempts to encompass the entire ritual world
within a single totality, a single horizon of
possibilities for sacred reality.

Catholic Pentecostalism and the Church

It is difficult to judge the depth beneath
the apparent unity of the movement in Latin America.
But if it is true, in Vallier's words, that "The
traditional Church throughout Latin America is
organizationally weak, hierarchically underdeveloped,
clumsily coordinated, split internally by special
interests and extraecclesiastical pressures, and
relatively incapable of using its legal framework
as an effective system of command and action" (1970:
28), at least two implications arise. First, the
movement may well easily achieve a great deal of
autonomy of action and doctrine within the Church,
lessening chances for tension with the hierarchy
that could result in schism. Second, the movement
may itself be an avenue for national and regional
integration within Latin American Catholicism.

The ideal of regional integration within the
Church under a charismatic banner is expressed in
the following statement by a participant in the

1976 leaders' conference: "We have for years been hearing about conferences, seminars, etc. to find the Caribbean Church, to localize the Church in the Caribbean, to have our Caribbean music and culture expressed in our church... THIS IS THE CARIBBEAN CHURCH". In assessing such assertions it must be recognized that as a plan for revitalization as well as a missionary strategy the movement is not without tools - organizational skills as well as the promise of enthusiastic religious experience to its members. Moreover, the potential for re-Catholicization of nominal adherents is considerable. The acceptance of faith-healing within the Catholic context means that non-Catholic (including Classical Pentecostal) healers can be dispensed with by those who formerly consulted them surreptitiously, and the recognition of evil spirits as real but defeatable provides a lever against syncretistic Afro-Christian cults, long in competition with orthodox Catholicism in parts of the Caribbean and Latin America.[17] The success of the Catholic Pentecostal retreat among the Mapuche Indians, discussed above, is a vivid example of the movement's potential impact in this respect.

Another important factor is that this movement offers a strictly religious solution to the problems of the Latin American Church. This is clear in the statement by a correspondent to the international newsletter: "What could not be done in the Caribbean politically or economically, that is, by the power of man, God seems to be doing through his Caribbean Church, especially through the movement of his Holy Spirit known as the charismatic renewal". The rejection of political action must be construed in light of another statement by a North American movement leader to the effect that the Charismatic Renewal is faced by a "head-on conflict with liberation theology" within the Church. For their part representatives of the latter position unhesitatingly define Catholic Pentecostal apoliticism as retreatism and abnegation of social responsibility.

The movement's missionary potential and its conservative stance suggest the manner in which it will appeal to various Catholic elites in Latin America. Vallier (1970) identifies four such elites. The old-line church 'politicians' are oriented to the power structure of secular society for support, protection, and legitimation, and reflect upper class sentiment. The 'papists' are militant moderns aimed at re-Christianizing the world from within the Church, and look directly to Rome for validation. While both these elites are oriented toward the <u>hierarchy</u>, two newer elites are oriented in terms of <u>co-operation</u> (1970:206). The 'pastors' aim is to build strong, worship-centered congregations, and their key words are 'co-operation, community, communication, pastoral care, the meaning of the sacraments'. The 'pluralists' are concerned with the Church as a "differentiated, grassroots agency of moral and social influence", and charge the 'pastors' with escapism, retreatism, and withdrawal. The Catholic Pentecostal strategy of renewing the Church from within places them squarely in the camp of the 'papists' with respect to the hierarchy. Their emphasis on interpersonal relations within tight-knit Christian communities places them on the side of the 'pastors' with respect to co-operation. This orientation would seem to situate Catholic Pentecostals midway between the political right and left wings of the Latin American Church: if Pentecostalism is rightly considered a 'third force' in Christianity after Catholicism and Protestantism, it may be that Catholic Pentecostalism will be a kind of political 'third force' within the Catholic Church. At the same time, the relative influence of the elites to whom the movement can be expected to appeal may serve as an indicator of its potential success in particular Latin American countries or dioceses.

Two Pentecostalisms

The co-presence of Pentecostalism and Catholic Pentecostalism in Latin America poses the sociological problem of differential appeal of two forms of what is ostensibly the same movement. A useful comparison can be made with La Ruffa's (1969; 1971) study of classical Pentecostalism in San Cypriano, a barrio of black Puerto Ricans in a very highly urbanized area on the coast of Puerto Rico fifteen miles east of San Juan. Here, contrary to developments in Aguas Buenas, classical Pentecostalism has flourished (although the majority of households remain nominally Catholic). The first two churches were founded in the 1930's and maintained a small membership until 1949. From 1949 to 1964 six new churches and campos were founded, adding up to a 400% increase in Pentecostal membership. This has occurred in the context of rapid industrialization and opportunities for substantial wage increases for some.

La Ruffa discusses the religious change in terms of reaction to stress caused by sociocultural change. He tentatively understands the emergence of a middle class (los comodos) as follows:

> It is my impression that this new structural feature - an emergent class system as a basis for the crystallization of status groupings - is an important consideration for the understanding of such feelings as inferiority and alienation. This kind of situation, it seems to me, involves individuals in interpersonal relations which can no longer be viewed exclusively in terms of kinship and neighborliness (1969:275).

The hypothesis implicit in this is that the alienation and inferiority experienced by those left behind as los pobres in the formation of a middle class predispose them to adopt Pentecostalism.[18] But what will be the religion of the rising middle class? To suggest that it might be Catholic Pentecostalism is also to suggest the versatility and adaptability of Pentecostalism as a cultural complex which can serve to crystallize status groups not only in the working class but in the middle and perhaps peasant classes as well.

Comparing the situations of Aguas Buenas and San Cipriano suggests that while classical Pentecostalism can gain a foothold in a certain segment of the population in localities where industrialization and proletarianization are most rapid and intense, Catholic Pentecostalism will have an advantage among a more 'respectable' urban middle class and in more conservative rural areas where a peasant life-style and nominal loyalty to Catholicism are intact.[19]

From a slightly different perspective it can be stated that while classical Pentecostalism appeals primarily to the struggling working class, Catholic Pentecostalism appeals precisely to an emerging middle class, which in turn brings along the very poor to the extent that relations of patronage are established through charity. The dual appeal of Catholic Pentecostalism is particularly evident in Mexico. There, both in Mexico City and Juarez, we have seen that Catholic Pentecostalism is the basis for alliance between very poor squatters and members of the middle class. This alliance is given a special ideological significance by participants' claims that it demonstrates the power of Catholic Pentecostalism to transcend the barriers between social and economic classes.

Yet the religion cannot be said to have <u>created</u> the structural link between the 'marginal' population and the middle class. Studies show pre-existing economic links in the production by squatters for the middle class of "services and homemade goods at costs below" those possible in the dominant sector of the economy (Perlman, 1976: 25). Such links are also evident in squatter community organization. In her Brazilian study Perlman reveals extensive connections between the squatters' own elite and the "supra-local agencies, the bureaucrats, politicians, architects, lawyers, and other high-status individuals possessing skills and resources relevant to the satisfaction of local needs" (1976:166). In this light, Catholic Pentecostalism might be understood as an ideological articulation of pre-existing socioeconomic relationships - an articulation both in the expressive sense of the religious value placed on 'transcending class and cultural barriers' in the name of Christianity, and in the instrumental sense of facilitating these relationships in practice. Conversely, the extent to which these interclass links are previously developed in a locale may facilitate the growth of Catholic Pentecostal groups.[20]

These formulations are supported by the evidence from Chile, where the two Pentecostalisms appear to have different bases of appeal both geographically and socially. Classical Pentecostalism is proportionately strongest in the south central provinces of Arauco, Concepción, Valdivia, Cautin, and Malleco (d'Epinay, 1969:23). According to d'Epinay, this heartland of Chilean Protestantism is also a stronghold of the working-class based communist movement. Catholic Pentecostalism is strongest among the middle class in the capital at Santiago and the urban poor in the Santiago suburb of Manuel Rodriguez, and in the traditional and isolated provinces of Atacama in the far north and Aysén in the far south. Where the two Pentecostalism are present simultaneously, as in the Mapuche region, classical Pentecostalism appeals to the more hispanized segment of the population (d'Epinay's informants acknowledge only that "we all have some Indian blood"), while Catholic Pentecostalism appeals to those with a more explicitly Mapuche identity.[21]

Aside from this class-based difference in appeal, Catholic Pentecostalism is differentiated from classical Pentecostalism by a greater degree of international organization. A key factor is the dominance of North Americans in the international expansion of the Catholic movement. It may be useful to conceive of the movement as a kind of 'religious multinational corporation', the influence of which parallels that of North American interests in the economic sphere. The community at Aguas Buenas in Puerto Rico could be regarded as the major Latin American 'subsidiary' of such a religious multinational.[22] Its former pastor, a native of the United States, was himself appointed in 1979 as chairman of the movement's newly formed International Council. The analogy takes on added significance in light of current interest in the 'world system' as a unit of social analysis (Wallerstein, 1974). Future research on Catholic Pentecostalism and religion in the world system would do well to take this into account.

Conclusion: What is Pentecostalism?

Three substantial facts have been presented in this discussion: 1) Catholic Pentecostalism is a basis for regional integration through its common forms of religious experience, its emphasis on tight-knit communities, and its periodic conferences which encourage the formation of a movement in Latin America includes the middle class and the 'very poor'; 3) Catholic Pentecostalism is in large part the result of an initiative from the United States, and is likely to be introduced where there is an active North American missionary presence. These facts provide a vantage for some general reflections on Pentecostalism as a social and religious phenomenon.

Pentecostalism is usually regarded as a source of motivation for economic action and social mobility. The problem with this hypothesis is that it is based only on theological doctrines of Baptism in the Holy Spirit, individual salvation, and a personal relationship with God, and thus assumes a highly individualistic ethos in Pentecostalism. When the social organization of Pentecostalism is examined, it becomes clear that the individual is often absorbed in a communalistic structure which demands a great deal of time for collective worship and considerable effort for mutual aid.[23]

Thus within Pentecostalism as a motivational system, the person can either be defined primarily as an individual or as a community member. Applied to the ethnology of Pentecostalism, this point could help account for some of the movement's internal diversity. In Chile, classical Pentecostal congregations are organized along the lines of traditional corporate groups, the pastor playing a role analogous to the colonial hacendado or the indigenous cacique (d'Epinay, 1969). By contrast, in Jamaica a 'progressive' and individualistic Pentecostalism was introduced by aspiring migrant workers returning from stints of labor in the United States (Wedonoja, 1980). In this light, the Catholic Pentecostal emphasis on community, while thoroughly Catholic in some respects, can also be seen as a development of a theme fundamental to Pentecostalism.

This is again a point about the adaptability of Pentecostalism to a variety of social situations. While in one case communal solidarity may relieve pressures for economic achievement, in another individual religious experience may support material aspirations. Given the alternative of emphasis on communal solidarity, there are two possible orientations, bound up with the Pentecostal disdain for the 'World' of vulgar affairs. First, communal solidarity and world-renunciation can orient action toward upward social mobility by reducing the fear of risk and anxiety about competition ("success and failure are merely worldly matters"). Second, it can encourage satisfaction with very little in the way of material goods and comforts. Either of these alternatives may in turn be expressed positively as ascesis or negatively as complacence. In the case of Catholic Pentecostalism, individual energies are channeled into service to the collectivity, and subordinated to the will of the collectivity by a tightly articulated system of authority. The community provides for the individual; it is the community as a whole that is motivated to achieve, but success is defined by progress toward the goal of the renewal of Christianity.

    The preceding discussion suggests a reevaluation of Pentecostalism as an object of study. Against the background of a highly Catholic Latin America, where Catholicism itself is open to a variety of syncretistic influences, Pentecostalism at first appears as a stubbornly discrete and self-consistent cultural entity. The impression is strengthened by the fact that in the United States this apparently monolithic entity has practically generated an independent field of 'Pentecostal studies.' However, especially since the advent of neo-pentecostalism in the 1950's, Pentecostalism seems to be anything and everywhere. It is organized into sect-like denominations, independent churches, and groups within main-line denominations. Assemblies of God, Nigerian Aladura churches, and Catholic Pentecostals thus all fall within the category of 'Pentecostalism'. Both working class and bourgeois elite are represented in the movement. Thus snake-handlers from the hollows of Appalachia can be ranged alongside sedate Episcopalians from well-to-do suburban parished. As a religious system, aside from the experience of 'Baptism in the Holy Spirit', none of the ritual elements - prophecy, faith-healing, glossalalia, laying on of hands, slaying in the Spirit (ritual dissociation) - are unique to Pentecostalism. For these reasons it could be proposed that the object of study be conceived not as a uniform and narrowly defined 'Pentecostalism', but as a widespread and diverse 'Pentecostal complex' that shares traits with other religious forms and whose main feature is adaptability to a variety of alien cultural contexts. Such a change in attitude may encourage a more open approach to this phenomenon than that dictated by the heretofore standard questions of the emotional stability of its practictioners or its role as a vehicle of social mobility.

Notes

1. Data for this discussion is drawn from movement publications, interviews with leaders, and from the <u>ICO Newsletter</u>, which was generously made available to me by the staff of the International Communications Office of the charismatic renewal.

2. Evidence suggests that the movement is typically introduced to a country by a priest or other religious, often a member of an order with a branch in the United States. The religious visits the USA, is exposed to the Baptism in the Holy Spirit, organizes a prayer group on his return, and subsequently calls on outside help for doctrinal instruction, healing services, or administration of the 'Life in the Spirit Seminar' (a widespread initiation rite that provides both indoctrination and a controlled setting for Baptism in the Holy Spirit). Perhaps a dozen major figures regularly make excursion to movement outposts. There is an apparent tendency for groups to maintain relations with the individual or group responsible for initial instruction and organizational assistance. Most ambitious among these groups is The Word of God in Ann Arbor, which as mentioned above has ties with communities around the globe. It has staged leaders' institutes in which delegates from all continents have visited the community for discussion and instruction.

3. Two developments in the Latin American Catholic Church have prepared the ground for an enthusiastic-communitarian Catholic Pentecostalism. <u>Los Cursillos de Cristianidad</u> (Little Courses in Christianity) consist of a three day period of spiritual awakening conducted by a team of priests and laymen, and aimed at cultivating a sense of community among participants. This movement was initiated by Bishop Juan Hervas of Ciudad Real, Spain, in 1949, whence it was introduced into Latin America and later into the United States (<u>New Catholic Encyclopedia</u>, vol.4:548). Many leaders

of Catholic Pentecostalism, in particular those most responsible for its international expansion, have previously been involved in Los Cursillos. Their reasons for shifting allegiance to the new movement are substantially the same as the list of weaknesses recognized in the Latin American Cursillos: 1) rapid diminishing of the original impulses; 2) primitive attachment to other Cursillistas in an attempt to perpetuate the original experience; 3) anomie and frustration regarding the nature of the task following training (Vallier, 1970:109). Catholic Pentecostals claim to resolve these difficulties by elaborating a mature model of Christian community following the Baptism of the Holy Spirit.

The second relevant development in Latin American Catholicism are the <u>Communidades de Base</u> (base communities). These parish renewal groups operate under the supervision of a pastor, but with largely lay leadership. Their aim is to "bring the laity up to date on the Church's teachings, to foster a sense of religious community, and to encourage laymen to integrate the ethical principles of Christianity to their secular acties" (Vallier, 1970:108).

4. The bishops included one Argentinian, two Guatemalans, one Panamanian, and four Mexicans.

5. Every country in Latin America has experienced some Catholic Pentecostal activity. Other developments worthy of note have taken place in the following places: Dominican Republic in the towns of Nagua and Pimentel (where a group is directed by a French Canadian missionary) and in the mountain region around Jarabacoa; Honduras in the towns of San Pedro Sula and El Mochito (where a covenant community appears to be emerging under American influence); Peru in the city of Negritos (where a group is directed by an American and an English priest); Trinidad-Tobago and Venezuela appear to have sizable contingents of Catholic Pentecostals. The movement appears to be slow

in gaining a foothold in the Latin American giants, Argentina and Brazil. The comparatively greater Europeanization of Argentina may be significant in diminishing the impact of the American movement (cf. Vallier, 1970:218), though the fairly large Argentine middle class could provide a sizable base of support in the long run. In Brazil, the movement has found itself in competition with Umbanda as Satanically inspired; Howe (1980) remarks that for this reason classical Pentecostalism and Umbanda are mutually exclusive in Brazil. Moreover, Umbanda apparently appeals to the same status groups as does Catholic Pentecostalism; Howe (1980) reports that Brazilian Pentecostals are predominantly of working class status, while Umbandists range from very poor to elite status (Howe's discussion of differential class appeal between Pentecostalism and Umbanda was one inspiration for the class-based analysis of Pentecostalism and Catholic Pentecostalism).

6. Urban-rural contrast in the population profile is revealed in the following table:

	unemployment	below pov. level	income above 10,000	median income
puebla	3.1%	51.4%	5.4%	$3935
municipio	9.1%	72.4%	3.7%	$2654
nat. avg.	5.6%	59.6%	10.3%	$3063

Source: U.S. Census, 1970

7. Of three grocers, three druggists, and three doctors in town, one each belongs to the CP group, in addition to the postmaster and the owner of the only movie theater, who no longer shows R-rated films. The actual extent of "middle class" participation is unknown. The U.S. Census records 169 proprietors of commercial and manufacturing establishments. Of the total population, 34.9% are either white collar or government employees.

8. The typical covenant community 'household' is a residential unit composed of one or more unrelated nuclear families and/or several unmarried people. The household 'head' is strictly responsible for the material and spiritual welfare of its members.

9. Squatter settlements in Mexico City are referred to either as 'lost cities' or as 'proletarian colonies', depending on one's politics. In 1969 an estimated 45% of the city's population resided in such communities (Perlman, 1976). Case studies have been published by Cornelius (1973) and Lomnitz (1977).

10. Ugalde's case study of one of the more affluent of these barrios somewhat surprisingly concludes that the only "real problem" is unemployment.

11. Manuel Rodriguez originated with the resettlement and union of several older settlements, including Jose Maria Caro, which in the early 1960's had a population of 120,000, or 18% of Santiago's total. The political union of the older communities was in part an effort by their residents to gain some degree of autonomy vis-a-vis the government (Portes and Ferguson, 1977:79, and personal communication).

12. In a statement similar to those from other national hierarchies (see McDonnell, 1976), the Cardinal made doctrinal clarifications, praised the spiritual life of the movement, and cautioned it against excesses, recommending that clergy take an informed interest and that participants not ignore the Eucharist and liturgy. The Bishop of Aysén, himself a member of the movement, emphasized prayer, doctrinal formation, establishment of local communities of committed lay people, apostolic work, the necessity of mature leadership, and cooperation with the <u>communidades de base</u>, while cautioning against "sensationalism, emotionalism, and elitism" in practice.

13. Seating in North American Catholic Pentecostal meetings is in concentric circles, and participants are not separated by sex.

14. Some Pentecostals engage in the practice of 'dancing in the Spirit'.

15. Note that the number of priests officiating was also four.

16. The retreat organizers apparently failed to recognize the equivalence and apparent incompatibility of the Mapuche use of the number four to symbolize totality, and the Christian use of the number three for the same purpose.

17. Fr. Francis MacNutt, O.P., a leading Catholic Pentecostal faith healer, made the following observation following a journey to Nigeria. Whereas in the United States the practices of faith-healing and deliverance from evil spirits emerged several years after the movement began, in Nigeria they could be "an integral part of introduction to the Charismatic Renewal... [to] introduce people to the power of God and convince them that they must no longer seek spiritual help from diviners and priests of the traditional religions" (1975:12). MacNutt believes that rather than rejecting the healing work of classical Pentecostals and indigenous healers as superstition, Catholics should be able to do the same work, only better.

18. Thus Pentecostalism provides healing from stress-related psychosomatic illness, aesthetic and emotional satisfaction, a sense of community and a means for attaining status within the group, a meaningful world view, and promotion of behavior compatible with (and adaptive to) the 'modern' trend of society (La Ruffa 1969:278-80).

19. Of course, it may be more simply that Catholic Pentecostalism becomes established wherever a pastor happens to have contact with the movement and becomes baptized in the Holy Spirit,

bringing his congregation along with him. First-hand comparative studies of localities such as San Cipriano and Aguas Buenas would help to resolve these questions.

20. Information on classical Pentecostalism in Mexico is scanty. All the present writer could find was Hollenweger's statement that, "In Mexico the Pentecostal movement has not very many members, but has had to brave severe persecutions..." (1972: 64).

21. Chilean Pentecostals customarily regard sects such as Jehovah's Witnesses and Mormons on the one hand and Roman Catholics on the other as equally unacceptable extremes; 87% of Pentecostal pastors regard Catholicism as excommunicated from the 'Body of Christ' (d'Epinay, 1969:170). A younger generation of Protestants appears to be less condemnatory, and if the example of the United States is followed, many will at least grudgingly accept the apparent incongruity of a pentecostalism within the Catholic Church.

22. Since 1972 it has sponsored retreats for Catholic Pentecostals from all of Latin America, as well as for elsewhere in Puerto Rico and the Caribbean. It helps sponsor the movement's annual Latin American leaders' conference (ECCLA), and publishes a monthly magazine.

23. La Ruffa records the total number of 'man-hours' devoted to religious participation in San Cipriano as 200 per week for Catholics as compared with 2800-3000 per week classical Pentecostals (1971:90). In this respect Catholic Pentecostals doubtless resemble classical Pentecostals more than their fellow Catholics.

Bibliography

Aldunate, Carlos
    1975 "Chile". ICO Newsletter 1:5:3.

Christopulos, Diane
    1974 "Puerto Rico in the Twentieth Century: A Historical Survey". In A. Lopez and J. Petras, eds., Puerto Rico and Puerto Ricans: Studies in History and Society, Cambridge: Schenkman Pub. Co.

Cornelius, Wayne
    1973 Political Learning among the Migrant Poor: The Impact of Residential Context. Beverly Hills: Sage Pub.

d'Epinay, Christian Lalive
    1969 Haven of the Masses: A Study of the Pentecostal Movement in Chile. London: Lutterworth Press.

Faron, Louis
    1964 Hawks of the Sun: Mapuche Morality and its Ritual Attributes. Pittsburgh: University of Pittsburgh Press.

Fenton, Jerry
    1969 Understanding the Religious Background of the Puerto Rican. Cuernavaca: Centro Intercultural de Documentacion.

Hollenweger, Walter
    1972 The Pentecostals: The Charismatic Movement in the Churches. Minneapolis: Augsberg Pub. House.

Howe, Gary Nigel
    1980 "Capitalism and Religion at the Periphery: Pentecostalism and Umbanda in Brazil". In S. Glazier, ed. Perspectives on Pentecostalism: Case Studies from the Caribbean and Latin America,

Washington: University Press of America.

La Ruffa, Anthony
1971 *San Cipriano: Life in a Puerto Rican Community*. New York: Gordon and Breach.

―――――
1969 "Culture Change and Pentecostalism in Puerto Rico". *Social and Economic Studies* 18:273-81.

Lomnitz, Larissa
1977 *Networks and Marginality: Life in a Mexican Shantytown*. New York: Academic Press.

MacNutt, Francis, O.P.
1975 "Report from Nigeria". *New Covenant* 4:11:8-12.

Mawn, Benedict
n.d. *Testing the Spirits*. Unpublished PhD. dissertation, Boston University, Sociology.

McDonnell, Kilian, O.S.B.
1976 *Charismatic Renewal and the Churches*. New York: Seabury Press

New Catholic Encyclopedia
1967 "Cursillo". (vol. 4) New York: McGraw-Hill.

Perlman, Janice
1976 *The Myth of Marginality: Urban Poverty and Politics in Rio de Janeiro*. Berkeley: U. Cal. Press.

Portes, Alejandro and D. Frances Ferguson
1977 "Comparative Ideologies of Poverty and Equity: Latin America and the United States". In Irving Horowitz, ed. *Equity, Income, and Policy: Comparative Studies in Three Worlds of Development*, New York:

Praeger.

Séguy, Jean
    1975 "Situation Socio-Historique du Pentecôstisme". In *Lumière at Vie*, special issue, *Le Mouvement Charismatique* 25:33-58.

Seromik, Gary
    1976 "The Gospel in Power". *New Covenant* 5:11:32-34.

Talavera, Carlos
    1976 "The Charismatic Renewal and Christian Social Commitment in Latin America". (p. 1 & 2) *New Covenant* 6:2 and 3.

Ugalde, Antonio
    1974 *The Urbanization Process of a Poor Mexican Neighborhood*. Austin: Institute of Latin American Studies, U. of Texas.

Vallier, Ivan
    1970 *Catholicism, Social Control, and Modernization in Latin America*. Englewood Cliffs: Prentice-Hall.

Wallerstein, Immanuel
    1974 *The Modern World-System*. New York: Academic Press.

Wedonoja, William
    1980 "The Pentecostal Movement in Jamaica". In S. Glazier, ed., *Perspectives on Pentecostalism: Case Studies from the Caribbean and Latin America*, Washington: University Press of America.

PENTECOSTALISM

Christianity and Reputation

Frank E. Manning

The recent interest of social scientists in Pentecostalism reflects both the growth of an intriguing religious phenomenon and the diminishment of a traditional intellectual bias against the study of fundamentalist Christianity. Much of this interest has been generated by anthropological research in societies where colonialism in one form or another has been a dominant influence, and where Pentecostalism--again, in one form or another--has been for several decades a dynamic force in local life. Nowhere is the vitality of Pentecostalism more striking than in the Caribbean and circum-Caribbean, a region where the conditions and circumstances of colonialism are played out daily in the tragicomic, almost farcical manner that prompted the native novelist V.S. Naipaul (1970) to call it the "Third World's third world." The region exemplifies, indeed caricatures, the sociocultural situations that help to make Pentecostalism an attractive system of meaning and style of life. Furthermore, Pentecostalism is appropriately viewed as what Clifford Geertz (1972) terms a "metasocial commentary"-- a symbolic production in which the participants discover, dramatize, and reflect upon the realities of their existence; what the cockfight tells us about Bali, the revival service can tell us about the Caribbean.

As this volume is addressed to the role of Pentecostalism in modernization, I will focus my prefatory remarks on a question that is of both human and analytic importance to that issue. Is Pentecostalism a vehicle of indigenous cultural symbols, an expression of native sentiments and interests? Or is it a vulgar Americanism that functions in favor of metropolitan values and imperial control? The contributors' answers throw light on the quality of relationship that Pentecostalism develops with recipient cultures and enable us to generalize about the religion's semantic and social influences in a region that is, loosely speaking, in the throes of modernization.

William Wedonoja's stand on the side of Pentecostalism as an indigenous cultural expression is clear and unabashed. While recognizing that the movement in Jamaica has American origins and affiliations, he contends that it has been reinterpreted in the context of the needs and aspirations of its Jamaican constituents. Pentecostalism speaks to the masses in their own language, and is a "truly revolutionary" religion.

Cornelia Flora's position with respect to Colombia is similar. She notes, for example, that when hymns are translated from English into Spanish, the tune takes on a Latin beat and different meanings are stressed. The Colombian church has a distinctly proletarian orientation, and its members understand Biblical verses such as "the first will be last and the last will be first" as heralding a confrontation with the power structure in which they will be helped by the Holy Spirit.

Frederick Conway's Haitian Pentecostals view American wealth as proof of American righteousness, but have nonetheless produced a version of their religion that is unmistakably Haitian and indeed closely comparable to Vodoun, the traditional animistic belief and ritual system in which an estimated nine-tenths of the population participate. The Holy Spirit is construed as similar but superior to the Vodoun loua, and Pentecostal services have the same performance elements and descriptive characteristics as Vodoun ritual. The parallel is particularly close in the New Word Church, which is part of a national Haitian organization with no metropolitan sponsor. Non-Pentecostal Haitians tend to believe that the New Word members are serving a loua who is only pretending to be the Holy Spirit.

Stephen Glazier notes that Trinidadian Pentecostals value their institutional ties with American churches, which are a means of financial support as well as a network that facilitates travel and immigration to the United States. The American connection also channels American values into sermon material, although such values are often alien to the warp and woof of Trinidadian society. On the other hand, the ludic theatrics and comic irony of the Pentecostal exorcism ritual that he describes--not to mention that the demons in question are creatures of Trinidadian folk mythology--make it clear that Pentecostalism has adapted to, and become a vehicle of, the creole culture. Just as Haitian Pentecostalism is viewed as more effective than Vodoun as an instrument of healing, Trinidadian Pentecostalism is regarded as a more salutary means of exorcism than that found in the Rada or Shango cults, or the private techniques of Obeahmen.

Dealing with Catholic Pentecostalism in Puerto Rico, Tom Chordas suggests metaphorically that the movement is a "religious multinational" in which the local church at Aguas Buenas is a subsidiary of the Word of God from Ann Arbor, Michigan. But he also points out that the Puerto Rican devotees modify American organizational and disciplinary dictates to suit their own cultural standards. More reflexively, Catholic Pentecostals throughout the region view their liturgy as an integration of traditional Christianity with Caribbean culture. In the words of a spokesman enthusiastically proclaiming the movement's identity, "This is the Caribbean Church."

Donna Birdwell and Judith Hoffnagel address the indigenous-metropolitan dichotomy with reference to social structural rather than cultural considerations. Comparing Pentecostalism to four other religions in a northern Belizean community, Birdwell observes that Pentecostalism draws its constituency primarily from those who are marginal to strong patrifamily units, whereas the other assemblies are built on patrifamilies. She argues that Pentecostalism is a substitute, organizationally and sentimentally, for the patrikin unit. Hoffnagel, who studied the Assembly of God in northeast Brazil, posits that the Pentecostal community is remarkably similar to the subordinate population on a plantation, and likens the pastor's role to that of the patrao (patriarchal family head) in terms of his absolute power and personalistic hold over the congregation. She contends that the growth of Pentecostalism corresponds only indirectly to industrialization and urbanization; a more direct cause is the disruption of the plantation and the extended family system, leaving a social vacuum into which Pentecostalism has easily moved. In both Birdwell's and Hoffnagel's cases, Pentecostalism resonates with traditional forms of social structure, not with the social formations that have emerged under recent metropolitan influences.

The papers of Anthony LaRuffa and Gary Howe differ from the others in arguing contrariwise that Pentecostalism is more in tune with foreign interests and ideologies than their indigenous counterparts. Speaking of Puerto Rico, LaRuffa holds that the accommodationist character of Pentecostalism fosters passive acceptance of existing conditions. Thus his informants favor the island's Commonwealth (read colonial) status vis-a-vis the United States, opposing national independence on the grounds that it would lead to Communist takeover. Political issues aside, there is a certain difficulty in squaring this contention with LaRuffa's thesis that Pentecostalism attracts those persons who have benefited least from the branch plant economy, and who find in the religion ersatz gratification for their relative deprivation. Given the Puerto Rican political economy, is not national independence as much a 'pie in the sky' as any of the promises of millenial religion? If so, why do Pentecostals warmly embrace one form of escapism and disdainfully reject the other?

Gary Howe's erudite analysis of Pentecostalism in Brazil proceeds from a question that is the inverse of those posed by his fellow contributors. He asks not why Pentecostalism has grown, but why its growth has been retarded to the extent that it has claimed no more than five per cent of the Brazilian population. He answers that the Pentecostal cosmos is fundamentally alien not only to traditional Brazilian religious orientations but also to the worldview supported by contemporary sociopolitical forces. Pentecostalism is an artifact of the Western capitalist system, and thus largely irrelevant and contradictory in a society that is "developing" as a peripheral dependency of this system rather than an integral part of it. A more credible response to contemporary Brazilian conditions comes from Unbanda, a new cult whose view of the universe is diametrically opposite to Pentecostalism and that has possibly been sampled by as many as four-fifths of Brazilians. The Umbanda cosmos emphasizes particularism rather than universalism, amorality rather than morality, power rather than principle - symbolic relations that closely suit the Brazilian political economy.

In sum, seven contributors stress that Pentecostalism resonates with indigenous symbols and interests, while two contend that it is essentially an alien metropolitan import. The controversy (which I have deliberately oversimplified) can be better illuminated if we put it aside for a moment and move to another level of the issue. Assuming that we social scientists make reasonably accurate diagnoses about the role of religion in society--and such an assumption, like any held by Pentecostals, rests ultimately on faith--the box score of our contributors forces a nagging question: why does Pentecostalism come in for so much condemnation from those who most strongly identify themselves as the enemies of colonialism, notably the new national elites and the newly radicalized clergy of the mainstream churches?

An answer can be gleaned from the St. Vincent-born author Orde Coombs. Posing the rhetorical question "Is Massa Day Dead?", he answers: "Massa Day, it seems, never ends in the West Indies. It only grows blacker" (1974:15). In other words, the old system of plantation society and colonial politics persists. The only change is one of personnel. Black replaces white and native replaces foreigner, but a ruling class still dictates to a subordinate majority, relating to them with contempt, condescension, and cynical paternalism.

To the new national bourgeoisie, Pentecostalism is a threat. It is the religion of the masses and, more than that, the source and symbol of their self dignity and sense of human equality. The new elite view Pentecostalism in much the same way that their predecessors viewed early Methodism and the array of Afro-Christian cults: as a challenge to authority. As Wedonoja suggests in the case of Jamaica, the elite reaction is to stigmatize Pentecostalism by associating it with the United States or other allegedly imperialist countries. (In parts of the eastern Caribbean, stigmatization comes through being associated with the Communists.)

The cultural meaning of this type of reaction lies in a symbolic structure discerned by Peter Wilson (1973). The structure is built on antithetical but dialectially related value systems known in many parts of the Caribbean as "reputation" and "respectability." Reputation is indigenous, philosophically egalitarian, and embodied primarily by males; respectability is metropolitan-derived, class conscious, and embodied primarily by females but partially internalized by men with age and social advancement. Wilson contends that this dual value order is found throughout the Caribbean and circum-Caribbean, including the Hispanic-Iberian areas. Indeed, it is aptly viewed as a specialized version of the general symbolic opposition between, in Victor Turner's (1969) terms, "communitas" and "structure." Reputation is communitas, respectability structure.

For Wilson, the source and rationale of respectability is the Christian church. He makes no denominational distinctions but posits a basic difference between Christianity and the syncretic cults. The latter, he proposes, are not related to respectability at all, but instead to reputation. Their appeal is sacred rather than social, they give full play to men and male values, they exalt native cultural styles and values rather than colonial norms, and they differentiate within a field of equals rather than stratify into a hierarchy of non-equals.

I accept this scheme, but amend it to put Pentecostalism on the side of reputation, with the cults, rather than on the side of respectability, with the mainstream Christian churches. Its decentralized and acephalous structure (Birdwell and Flora), its heightened sense of equality and comaraderie (Chordas and LaRuffa), its playful orientation (Glazier), its emphasis on the mystical accrual of power (Conway), its indigenous reflexivity (Chordas)--all are basic indicators of reputation. Moreover, the overall ritual style of Caribbean Pentecostalism is built on competitive performance, an expressive tropism that is fundamental to reputation. As in many of the syncretic cults, this tropism is projected onto the behavior of the gods, creating a deus ludens to entertain and inspire homo ludens. A memorable example occurred during my early fieldwork in Bermuda (Manning 1977), when a Pentecostal pastor concluded an evangelical service by asking for a round of applause for God the Father. Anticipating what was to follow, the congregation clapped with restraint. Next he asked for applause for God the Son, and the response was similar. Finally he asked for applause for God the Holy Ghost, and there followed a standing, cheering, shouting ovation that lasted a quarter of an hour.

Looking to the future, one might predict that Pentecostalism will become increasingly more indigenous, particularly on the symbolic/cultural level. As this happens Pentecostalism will sever its ties with metropolitan sponsors, as has already happened in Haiti (Conway) and may happen in Jamaica, where those ties are less prestigious than the indigenous ones (Wedonoja). The model for this type of evolutionary (involutionary?) development has been set by such contemporary cults as Jamaican Pocomania and Trinidadian Spiritual Baptism, both of which had their initial inspiration in the nineteenth century from American Protestantism but later syncretized with Afro-creole residues. In another century Pentecostalism may join the Caribbean's syncretic cults--an eventuality that will add to Herskovits' (1958) stature and undoubtedly send new waves of anthropology students into the region. Indeed, if Wedonoja is right that there is a general "Pentecostalization" of Caribbean religion, Pentecostalism could be a vehicle for the rise of reputation over respectability--a process that Wilson (1973) sees as the concomitant of an authentic decolonization. The appeal of Catholic Pentecostalism to the middle class may signal this process, especially if Chordas is correct in arguing that the movement promotes a sense of creole identity as well as a sense of spiritual solidarity that transcends--or at least crosscuts--the traditional class hierarchy. To entertain a millenial dream--and here that is surely fitting--Massa Day could really be done, not simply darkened.

To return to the present, why are there such striking differences between LaRuffa and Howe, on the one hand, and the rest of the contributors, on the other? An important part of the answer, I think, lies in the ethnographic and analytic perspectives that are employed. LaRuffa focuses on the poverty of Puerto Rican Pentecostals and follows the classic Marxist-Freudian line that religion encourages an illusory escape from that situation, as opposed to an activist response to it. Howe's approach is more complex, deriving from his contention that the most significant feature of Pentecostalism is its general vision of the cosmos--a vision predicated on 1) the individualization of religious action, 2) the consolidation of religious power into a more or less unitary godhead, and 3) the objectification of a coercive and intrusive religious order articulated through universal rules. On this level of abstraction Pentecostalism is theologically Protestant, socially respectable, and, as Howe convincingly argues, incongruent with the political economy and culture of Brazil.

But is the Protestant cosmology what is really important and centrally meaningful about Pentecostalism? The other contributors answer negatively, but with different voices. Glazier and Conway deal with the ritual side of Pentecostalism, focusing respectively on its role in exorcism and healing. Wedonoja highlights the ethos of democratic egalitarianism. Hoffnagel, Birdwell, and Flora see Pentecostalism as a communal alternative to more rigid institutional complexes, notably the family. Pentecostalism is clearly many things, but to view it primarily as an expression of the Protestant cosmology is to miss a fundamental point: that most Pentecostals consciously choose their religion because of its perceived differences from other versions of organized Christianity, rather than its similarities to them.

The limits of the Protestant-Pentecostal comparison bear directly on the question of modernization. Weber (1958) argued that classical Protestantism encouraged modernization not simply because it contained particular beliefs and values that were conducive to socioeconomic reform/

rationalization, but also, and more importantly, because it promoted a total pattern of life aimed at relentless, systematic striving for ethical imperatives and the assurance of salvation in a world to come. Pentecostalism, by contrast, produces salvation in a single instant: the moment of conversion. It fosters a life pattern that is more episodic than methodic, more ritualistic than rational (Peacock 1971). Its concern with healing and exorcism indicates an accommodation to the "magic" that classical Protestantism viewed as a loathed vestige of Catholic sacramentalism and as a detraction from the serious and continuous pursuit of rational ideals.

Were Pentecostalism more like the classical Protestant stereotype, it would either radically change undeveloped societies, or, more likely, be so unsuited to them that it would quickly disappear or be relegated to unimportance. But this is not the case. Pentecostalism is a structurally loose and variable enough set of symbols that it can be selectively assimilated into many different types of non-Western societies. The result is a religion that wields discrete modernizing influences (through the emphasis on sober living, self-improvement, etc.) but that in its overall form becomes an expression of the native ethos, a symbol of reputation. Not surprisingly, much of the upward mobility that Pentecostals display results from opportunistic means such as the exploitation of personal networks (LaRuffa), rather than the methodical and relentless hard work that impressed Weber in classical Protestantism.

There is now emerging, as Chordas suggests, a field of "Pentecostal Studies." This volume is a seminal entry in that field, which promises to contribute a great deal to both the social science of religion and the ethnology of modernization.

References Cited

Coombs, Orde, ed.
1974 *Is Massa Day Dead?*
Garden City, N.Y.: Doubleday Anchor.

Geertz, Clifford
1972 "Deep Play: Notes on the Balinese Cockfight."
Daedalus 101, 1: 1-38.

Herskovits, Melville
1958 *The Myth of the Negro Past.*
Boston: Beacon Press

Manning, Frank
1977 "The Salvation of a Drunk."
American Ethnologist 4, 3: 397-412.

Naipaul, V.S.
1970 "Power to the Caribbean People."
New York Review of Books, September 3, 32-34.

Peacock, James
1971 "The Southern Protestant Ethic Disease" in J. Kenneth Morland, ed., *The Not So Solid South.*
Athens: University of Georgia Press, 108-113.

Turner, Victor
1969. *The Ritual Process.* Chicago: Aldine.

Weber, Max
1958 *The Protestant Ethic and the Spirit of Capitalism.*
Trans. Talcott Parsons. New York: Scribner's.

Wilson, Peter
1973 *Crab Antics.* New Haven: Yale University Press.

CONTRIBUTORS

DONNA BIRDWELL-PHEASANT received her Ph. D. in Anthropology from Southern Methodist University.

THOMAS J. CHORDAS earned his B. A. in Social Science from Ohio State University and his Ph. D. in Anthropology from Duke. In addition to his work on Pentecostalism, he has conducted folklore research in Hungary.

FREDERICK J. CONWAY studied Anthropology at Yale and American University. He conducted fieldwork in Haiti from 1974 to 1979, and is currently Assistant Professor of Anthropology at American University in Washington, D. C.

CORNELIA BUTLER FLORA received her Ph. D. from Cornell. She is a director of the Ford Foundation in Latin America and has taught at Kansas State University. Among her publications is: Pentecostalism in Colombia: Baptism by Fire and Spirit (Fairleigh Dickinson, 1976).

STEPHEN D. GLAZIER studied Anthropology at Princeton and the University of Connecticut where he earned his Ph. D. He conducted research in Trinidad from 1976 to 1979, and is currently Lecturer in Anthropology at the University of Connecticut, Storrs.

JUDITH CHAMBLISS HOFFNAGEL received her Ph. D. in Anthropology from Indiana University. She is presently affiliated with the Universidade Federal de Pernambuco.

GARY NIGEL HOWE is Assistant Professor of Sociology at the University of Kansas.

ANTHONY L. LARUFFA earned his Ph. D. from Columbia University, and is currently Professor of Anthropology at City University of New York (Lehman College). His book,

San Cipriano: Life in a Puerto Rican Community, was published in 1972.

FRANK E. MANNING received his Ph. D. from the University of North Carolina , and is currently Professor of Anthropology at the University of Western Ontario. He has done fieldwork in several Caribbean societies, combining studies of religion with a wide variety of other ethnological inquiries.

LUISE MARGOLIES earned her Ph. D. at Columbia University. She is presently a Research Associate at the Instituto Venezolano de Investifaciones Cientificas.

WILLIAM WEDENOJA is Assistant Professor of Anthropology at Southwest Missouri State University. His Ph. D. is from the University of California at San Diego.

NAMES

Aberle, David, 107 108
Adams, Richard N. 96,108
Aldunate, Carlos, 156,173
Amonker, Ravindra, 45
Anderson, Bo, 134, 138
Angrosino, Michael V. 71,78

Balan, Jorge, 138
Barber, Bernard,107, 108
Barrett, Leonard, 28, 46
Basileiro, Ana Maria 138
Beaubrun, Michael, 77
Beck, Jane C. 69,78
Berger, Peter, 76,78
Bingle, E. J. 50,65
Birdwell-Pheasnat, Donna, 2,4,95-109, 179,183,185
Brown, Diana, 128, 130, 138
Burkhart, Geoffrey, 25

Caldeiro, C. 138, 139
Calley, Malcolm, 28, 46
Camargo, C. P. P. de 130,139
Candido, A. 138,139
Cardoso, F. H. 134, 138
Carr, Andrew T. 77
Carroll, Michael P. 85,93

Chordas, Thomas P. 79,143-175,183, 184,186
Christopolous, Diane 147,173
Cockroft, James D. 134,138
Conway, Frederick J. 2,3,4,7-26,178, 184,185
Coombs, Orde, 182,187
Cornelius, Wayne, 170 173
Coser, Lewis, 71,78
Coxhill, H. W. 51,65
Curry, Donald E. iii, 122,123

Davis, J. Merle, 50, 65
Desmangles, Leslie iii.
Durkheim, Emile,126, 139
d'Epinay, Christian Lalive, 157,158, 163,165,172,173

Faron, Louis, 156, 157,173
Fenton, Jerry, 150, 173
Ferguson, D. F. 170, 174
Flora,Cornelia B. 2,4,81-93,178, 183,185
Frank, A. G. 126, 129
Freilich, Morris, 71,78
Fry, Peter, 128, 139

Furtado, C. 132, 139

Geertz, Clifford, 179,187
Gerlach, Luther P. 4,5,17,24,26,42, 43,46,105,109
Girdner, Linda, 25
Glazier, Stephen D. vii. 2,3,4,67-80, 179,183,185
Goodman, Felicitas D. iii. 77
Graham, L. S. 131, 138,139
Grubb, K. 50,51, 65
Guimarases, A. M. Z. 127,139

Haines, David, 25
Halpern, Katherine 25
Henney, Jeannette H. 28,46
Herskovits, Melville J. 28,47,68,78,184
Hine, Virginia, 17,26, 42,43,46,105,109
Hoffnagel, Judith 1,4,111-124,179,180, 185
Hogg, Donald, 28,47
Hollenweger, Walter, 172, 173
Howe, Gary Nigel, 2, 125-140,169,173,180,181,184, 185
Hutchinson, Bertram, 113, 123

Inkles, Alex, 75,76,78

Johnson, Benton, 71,78

King, Morton, 69, 78

LaBarre, Weston, 107, 109
LaRuffa, Anthony L. 28,47,49-65,149,150, 161,171,172,174,180, 184,185,186
Leal, V. N. 138, 140
Leeds, Anthony,131,140
Leonard, E. G. 138,140
Lerner, Daniel,56,92, 93
Lomnitz, Larissa, 170, 174
Linton, Ralph, 107,109

MacNutt, Francis, 171, 174
Manning, Frank E. 77, 177-187
Margolies, Luise, 1-5, 77
Mauss, Marcel, 126,137, 139,140
Mawn, Benedict, 143, 174
McClelland, David, 91,93
McDonnell, Kilian, 170,174
Medina, J. 112,123
Melvin, D. 111
Metraux, Alfred, 28, 47
Minz, Sidney, 7,26
Mischel, Frances, 28, 47,68,79
Moore, Joseph G. 28, 47
Murray, Gerald F. 8, 26

Naipaul, V. S. 177, 187

Niehoff, Arthur, 69,78

Parsons, Talcott 137,140
Peacock, James, 186 187
Perlman, Janice, 162, 170,174
Pierson, Donald, 138, 140
Pinto, R. S. 138, 140
Pollak-Eltz, Angelina iii. 3,5,68,71,76, 77,79
Portes, Alejandro,170, 174
Pressel, Esther,128, 140

Queiroz, M. I. P. de 127,132,141

Read, W. R. 111,122, 123,128,141
Redfield, Robert, 97 109
Reed, Nelson, 96,109
Reicher, Henry W. 25
Robotham, Hugh,31 47
Rodman, Hyman, 71, 79
Rosen, David, 25
Rycroft, W. S. 71, 79

Schacter, Stanley, 25
Séguy, Jean,144, 175
Seromik, Gary, 175
Sereno, Renzo, 67, 79

Shirley, R. W. 138, 141
Simpson, George Eaton 28,47,68,79
Spiro,Melford, 45
Smith, D. H. 75, 76, 78
Smith, M. G. 69,79

Talavara, Carlos, 152, 175
Tidrick, Gene, 33,48
Torrey, E. Fuller, 73, 80
Turner, Victor W. 73, 80, 183,187

Ugalde, Antonio,152, 170,175
Vallier, Ivan, 158, 160,168,169,175
Vergolino e Silva, A. 131,141
Villa Rojas, Alfonso, 97,109

Wallace, Anthony F. C. 107,109
Wallerstein, Immanuel 81,93,132,141,175
Ward, Colleen, 77,80
Weber, Max, 75,76,185-87
Wedenoja, William, vii. 4,71,76,80,165,175, 178,182,184
Willems, Emilio,28,48, 111,113,123,127,141
Williams, J. 69,80
Wilson, Bryan, 36,48, 122,123
Wilson, Peter J. 182, 187

Yawney, Carole, 71, 80
Young, Lloyd R. 45

SUBJECTS

Aggression,39
Aladura,166
Anomie,34,168
Antilles Episcopal Conference,144
Anti-Vodoun Campaigns, 11
Anti-Sorcery Movements 28
Appalachia,166
Apostolic Church,45
Assembly of Christian Churches,54

Bali,177
Banking,83
Baptists,45,49,52 122
Bauxite,33
Bethel Pentecostal Church,51
Bethesda Assembly 18,22
Bishop Juan Herras, 167
Bishop of Aysén, 153
Bon-Dieu,10,12,23
Boundary-Maintenance, 86,87
Brazil,1,2,28,82,111-141,180,181
Brooklyn,146
Brujeria,150

Caguas,55,59,196
California,50
Canada,70,84,144, 168
Canary Islands,144
Carmelite Nuns,145
Catholicism, 8,16,18, 21,49,68,91,92,100, 102,103,106,121

Charisma,22,143
Chihuahua,150
Chile,82,99,100,153, 163,165
Chinese,33,67
Cholchol,154,155
Christadelphians,101
Christian Missionary Church, 52
Church of England,45, 46,49,166
Church of God,29,52, 54
Church of the First Born, 32
Church of the Nazarene, 100
City Mission,32
Clarendon (Jamaica),31
Coffee,83
Collections,59
Colombia,2,59,81-94
Communists,182
Conservatism,42,118, 121
Conversion,14,15,21
Copiapó,154
Corregimientos,81
Corruption,136
Cotton,99
Cuba,60
Curepe, 68,72

Dancing in the Spirit 171
Denmark,84
Dependency Theory vii. 24
Dominican Republic, 54,145,168
Durango,150

East Indians,33,67
Ecology,29

England,28,84
Etiology of Disease, 9,39,76
Europe,126
Exorcism,72-76,179
Extra-Marital Activities,116

Faith Healing,2,4,14,16, 23,85,153,154,159
Family Ties,2,23,24,34, 40,82,84,92,104,106, 135,149
Folk Catholicism, 97, 98,101,127,131
France, 7,11

Gaitan,82
Galeria,88,89
German Lutheran Church,122
Glossolalia,13-16, 22,30,32,46,84, 85,122,157,166
Gold,83
Gossip,114
Great Revival,29
Guatemala,101,144,168

Haiti,7-26,144
Holy Cross Fathers,154
Holy Spirit,41,49,85, 122,143,144,146, 157, 166,171
Honduras, 102,144,168
Household Size,56,170
Hurricane,98,101
Hymns,85

Income,56,58,86,89
Industrialization, 4,24,33,113
Inner-Directed, 35
Iemanjá,131

Jamaica,27-48,165,178
Jehova Witnesses,172

Justicia y Alabanza, 151

Konvéti,14

Latifundia,82
Liberation Theology, 159
Los Angelos, 50

Machismo,148
Mahogany,98,99
Malaria,16
Manchester Parish,31
Mapuche Indians, 154-156,159,163,171
Maryknoll Fathers,153
Mass Media,92
Mayas,97,98,101
Medical Doctors,73
Mestizo,97
Metasocial Commentary, 177
Mexico City,150,151, 162
Migration,2,83,87,120
Minifundia,82
Modernization,23,27,34, 37,38,125
Monoculture,127
Mormons,172
Municipios,81

National Health Care 117
Nepotism,20,131
Newark,71
New Testament,19,30, 38
New York City,51
New York Times,51
Nigeria,.166
Novena,97

Obeah,67,69,73,75,76, 179
Old Testament,30,38

Palmira, Valle de Cauca, 81,88
Pennsylvania,70
Personal Values,3
Peru,153,168
Philadephia,71
Pilgrimages,73,76
Plantation Society,4, 27,112,114
Pluralism, 128
Politics,89,118
Pope Gregory the Great,155
Pope Paul IV,144
Population Loss,2
Port-of-Spain,72,74
Power,96,105
Presbyterians,46,49, 70,122
Prestige,34,36
Proletarianization, 81,91,92
Pukkumina,28

Rada,70
Rancheros,97,98
Rastafarians,28
Recife,114,118,120
Reciprocity,2
Redemptrists,146
Relative Deprivation, 85
Religious Evolution, 37
Reputation,182,183,186
Respectability,182, 183
Revitalization Movements 40
Revivalism,28,30,32

Saints,3,97,127,130
Santander,88
Santiago,153,154
Silver,83
Sin,24
Slavery,27

Solidary Groups, 86
Sorcery,38
Spiritual Baptists, 70,184
Squatters,151,162,170
Syncretism,28,68,166

Testimonies,73,86
Third World,42,44,125, 132,136,137,177
Tijuana,150
Tolima,88
Trance,8,13,14,29,122, 129,166
Trinidad,67-80,168,179

Umbanda, 125,128,129
United Pentecostal Church,85
United States,18,35,83, 84,99,144,164,180, 182
Urbanization,24,34,120

Venezuela,3,67,71,72, 144
Vodoun,4,8,10,28,29
Voting,89,119

War of a Thousand Days 82,83
Water Strikes,87
Wesleyan Movement,49
West Africa,24,27,36
Women as Converts, 21
Women in Organizational Hierarchy, 22
Word of God, 147,149,153, 154,167,179
World Rejection, 125

Yucatan,96